Rachel,

Do ahead and make
a difference

God Bless.

9-7-16

Replace Your Mortgage

How to Pay Off Your Home in 5-7 Years on Your Current Income

Michael Lush and David Dutton

ISBN: 978-1532880445

To request copies of this book please visit www.ReplaceYourMortgage.com or call 1-615-925-3887.

Comments From Clients

"...and it's saving me thousands of dollars on interest payments which is thousands of dollars that I keep in my pocket that the bank doesn't have."

Doug Krull, Hendersonville, Tennessee

"You don't have to change what you are doing today, as long as you are a little disciplined and you can set yourself up to be financially free just based on the fact that you are not tying yourself to a thirty year payment."

Brian McManus, Milwaukee, Wisconsin

"I eliminated my fixed amortized bank debt on my primary residence two years ago ($385K to zero in three years) using the principles outlined by RYM.
What was missing was knowledge and guidance to go beyond my primary residence and eliminate the debt on my rental properties. Non owner occupied lines of credit are very hard to find....thus RYM was exactly the missing link to bridging that gap and executing income property debt elimination....thus subsequent purchased of more income assets.
Without RYM, I would have not been able to blueprint and or execute such an outcome."

Captain Michael Murray, Los Angeles, California

Take Our Free Class

- **The Banking Scam:** Find out how the banks actually make their money off of the consumer and why leaving money in your checking account is one of the worst things you can do financially.
- **Hidden Mortgage Costs:** Discover how mortgages work and why your 15-30 year mortgage is costing you tens of thousands of dollars more than your home loan should.

VISIT

www.ReplaceYourMortgage.com/free

Contents

INTRODUCTION

"If people understood the banking system, there would be a revolution by morning. *- Henry Ford.*

If you are like me, you have looked at your mortgage statement and seen that regularly making those monthly payments barely makes a dent in the principal balance. I feel your pain. Fortunately, you are about to discover a proven method of paying off your home in an average of five to seven years, using only your current income.

This method is not on trial. The evidence is in, and it works! What is on trial is whether you will actually put this information to work and set your family free from debt. How are we so confident? It's simple. It is math, not magic. We didn't create math.

WHO THIS WORKS FOR

If you are a current homeowner or potential homeowner who does not want debt to dictate your flexibility, this is for you. Ideally, you will have at least 10% equity and a minimum credit score of 640. While these figures are optimal, we have found several banks that do not require any equity! Some people can actually purchase a new home with what we teach. You should be cash flow positive, meaning your income exceeds your expenses.

If you see yourself in the description above, why wait any longer to begin? This method has worked for millions of others, and it will work for you as well!

WHAT THIS METHOD IS NOT

This method is NOT…

- an illegal scam or a "trick"
- a HARP loan, streamline refinance, or any other traditional mortgage product; or
- a tool reserved for the wealthiest among us.

This method uses a little known but long-standing financial product called the home equity line of credit (HELOC). Don't mistake this for a home equity loan, which is just as bad as a mortgage.

Before you begin this journey, I would ask that you suspend your disbelief until you have allowed us to show you proof that this method works faster than any other method. That includes making biweekly payments or making an extra mortgage payment per year.

First, let's talk about how this journey began for me.

CHAPTER 1
Confession: The Case Against a Traditional Mortgage From a 14 Year Recovering Mortgage Banker

This book has been a long time coming and quite honestly, it's scary to put myself out there like this. However, if I am going to teach you to pay off your home in five to seven years, you should know a bit more about my background and how I came to this point in my life.

My name is Michael Lush, and for 14 years I have been a recovering Mortgage Banker. It has been a tough road to sobriety. My addiction to offering mortgage products started January 19th, 2002. I was young and fairly fresh out of college when a buddy of mine asked me to consider selling mortgages to folks as a career.

Don't get me wrong; it wasn't what you typically perceive as an addiction. This was no bunch of junkies in an alleyway getting high on an illegal substance. In fact, it was centered in a very nice office in a high-rise in downtown Charlotte, North Carolina, where I worked for the ninth largest lender in the country.

Looking back, this was a perfectly legal white collar position selling financial crack to homeowners. No one, including myself, thought we were doing anything wrong by offering homeowners a way to save money by refinancing their existing mortgages. I must add that although this was at the height of the subprime days, we weren't offering loans that put folks in a worse situation. Every loan I sold left folks in a much better position than they'd been in before they met me.

It didn't take long for me to get hooked. In a selfish way, I enjoyed making my borrowers happy. To top it off, the commission checks weren't bad. I was making more money than I knew what to do with, and it showed.

In my first year, I was pulling in $40,000 checks and had to get another fix quick because the money was gone faster than it came in. The same year, I was named "Newcomer of the Year". In my second year, I was promoted. Then promoted again and again. Just like any junkie, I was splurging on material items: a large home, several high end cars, and motorcycles. My wedding cost more than most people make in a year.

I say this not to brag, but out of embarrassment. I moved further away from the principles my parents instilled in me and further away from my faith. I never thought the supply of money would end, and just assumed this would be our life for the foreseeable future.

However, God had other plans, and he found the perfect opportunity to teach me a lifelong lesson…the housing crash! On my birthday, my family's employer--one of the largest lenders in the nation--filed bankruptcy. In a split second, all of my income came to a screeching halt.

Thankfully, I didn't do everything wrong. I had maxed out my 401k every year, and it performed extremely well. The majority of my 401k had been in company stock, which had gone from $0.02 a share to over $13. I had seen the writing on the wall and cashed in just before the value plummeted, giving me a healthy nest egg to live on for quite some time.

I knew that nest egg wasn't going to last forever, so I jumped back into the mortgage business, starting from the ground up again. Although I had finished with the last firm as a top sales manager, I had to start as a loan officer at another firm in Tennessee where no one knew my abilities as a leader. This was another one of God's perfect plans for me.

It humbled me and forced me to appreciate what I had squandered. My wife and I had to adopt a more realistic budget and financial plan to get back on our feet. I was always good at math, so my wife had me count the grocery bill plus taxes during our weekly trip to the grocery store. Times were tough and luxuries were non-existent, but it forced me to realize what was truly important in life: faith and relationships.

It was tough making a decent living in the mortgage industry after 2007, so I picked up some side jobs laying tile with a buddy of mine. Manual labor can teach you what "hard work" really means, and it made me appreciate once again how blessed I was to be given such an opportunity. I was no stranger to hard work. My parents had modeled a strong work ethic throughout my young life. I even found that the habits of working hard as an athlete poured over into my professional life.

One day, the former CEO of that ninth largest lender called, saying they were starting back up and wanted me to spearhead operations of a Nashville location. During my tenure with this firm, Nashville had been the black sheep of the company and the worst performer. In its previous life, the company had not been able to recreate the success it was having nationwide in Nashville.

However, I didn't second guess this opportunity and made a split second decision to say "yes" and become the Director of Operations for the resurrected firm. I started with four friends in a small office and within two years became the top branch and manager, growing the Nashville location to more than 60 employees and generating more than $20 million per month. I will freely admit I didn't achieve this alone. I hired folks I could trust who had talent that made up for my shortcomings.

Hard work leads to success and the money supply grew again. This time, we were going to do it right. My wife and I still lived as if we were poor. Our first major purchase was a vehicle: a 5 year old Jeep Commander with a lot of miles. It's sitting in the driveway to this day. For a while, we had lived with one car, and getting this additional vehicle allowed my wife to have a social life again. After another year, we decided it was time to buy a home again and stop throwing away our money on rent. We saved up a nice down payment for the home we still live in today.

Prior to buying the home, we spent several years without the luxury of TV. We entertained ourselves with books. I read mostly self-help and inspirational books. I decided to surround myself with folks who had what I wanted and engage in conversations I wanted to be a part of.

I realized that experience is a long and hard teacher, but I wanted to speed up the process. So, I invested in mentors, wealthy mentors. Being in the mortgage business, where compensation is tied to volume, I made an effort to gain the business of my mentor and his friends. They bought large homes and I wanted to be their mortgage banker. That led to enlightenment about what I was selling countless folks every day.

In an effort to earn their business and gain large mortgage transactions, I asked my mentor to introduce me to his friends. This is how it went:

Me: "If you could introduce me to your friends, I would greatly appreciate it, as I can provide them with mortgage solutions to fit their needs."

Mentor: "Michael, I don't mind introducing you but you will never get their mortgage business."

Me: "Why is that? I am good at what I do and can help them."

Mentor: "Michael, we don't get mortgages."

Me: "Let me guess, you pay cash for everything? Well, I have an answer for that too. Have you thought about the opportunity cost of using cash to buy things instead of leveraging the bank's money and retaining tax deductions?"

Mentor: "Yes we have Michael, but we don't use mortgages…we use lines of credit for businesses and homes."

Me: "Why in the world would you do that? Isn't that just like having a credit card on your home?"

See, I had spent years refinancing folks out of home equity lines of credit, telling them it was just like having a large credit card on their homes. In fact, I had refinanced the HELOC on my own Charlotte home into a traditional mortgage, thinking I was doing the right thing.

And that's when his next words hit me like a ton of bricks.

Mentor: "Mortgages are the most expensive and least efficient debts one can have. However, using a line of credit properly allows us to pay very little interest and pay off the debt VERY fast. We pour our cash flow into a HELOC, allowing simple interest to work in our favor just like businesses do. You can supply us with HELOCs and that would be an opportunity for you to get our business."

Some would ask if this conversation was a positive experience for me. Long term, the answer is an emphatic, "YES!" Short-term, this was a crushing blow. I had spent my entire career in the mortgage industry thinking I was doing the right thing, only to discover that I was doing the opposite. Ignorance was not an excuse for me.

Well, my company didn't offer HELOCs. Quite frankly, I didn't know jack about them. But I was about to buy a home. If they had a better solution, I wanted to benefit from their techniques. So, I spent a long time researching the topic. I spent long nights watching videos, making calls to financial planners and CPA's, and exploring other resources.

He was right! It is a much better strategy. All this time, I'd thought I was offering the best service and products to my customers, but really all I'd been doing was making the banks rich. Making my mentor and his friends rich. Heck, some of his friends owned mortgage companies, and the revenue was insane.

Did you read your Truth-in-Lending disclosure (now called a Loan Estimate)? Basically, you buy one home for you and another one for the bank. No wonder they loved soldiers like me. I sold their financial crack to middle class folks, which kept them coming back for more because the mortgages kept them in financial bondage for decades.

When rates dropped, most folks were chasing low rates to lower their mortgage payments, but also extending their terms back out again. It didn't matter that the rate was lower as long as the term was longer. The banks and mortgage companies made even more money! Money made off the backs of hardworking Americans.

Fast forward to my home today. I refinanced it into a HELOC shortly after I purchased it and started implementing what I thought of as my mentor's strategy. However, it wasn't his strategy. The concept and formula had been around for a century. Millions of folks outside of the U.S. had been doing this for a long time.

In fact, more than 80% of home buyers in Australia and the UK have been using this strategy since 1994. The strategy spread like wildfire, and those folks were paying their homes off in five to seven years on the same level of income. The strategy didn't require them to make more money or live on a tight budget.

In fact, all they did was change where their cash goes. Since a HELOC was open-ended, meaning money could go in and out freely, folks would put all their money into a HELOC, bypassing their checking accounts. When they needed to pay bills, they just used their HELOC to make a payment. As long as they made more money than they spent, the acceleration of this simple interest tool was astounding-- almost too good to be true if you didn't understand the simple math.

It's important to understand how banks make money. We give banks our money in the form of checking accounts. These accounts pay very low rates of return…0.17% on average! Then, when we need money for homes, cars, credit cards and such, the bank lends our money back to us at much higher rates. It's called turn or yield. To top it off, inflation rates are higher than the rate of return on checking and savings accounts, essentially making these accounts liabilities.

The easiest way to fix this is to stop leaving money in a checking account and instead to dump all funds into a HELOC. The more funds you put into it, the lower the payments become each month, since the interest is calculated on that day's principal balance. The lower the balance, the lower the payment. This allows more funds to go towards principal, creating a "debt reduction snowball".

You're probably asking yourself, "Why not just refinance to a 10 year mortgage?" Although that would help eliminate a lot of interest on your mortgage, it's still slower than using a HELOC cash flow strategy. And, dumping all of your funds into a closed-end mortgage means you just put your money into the bank's treasure chest with only two options for getting it back:

1. An expensive refinance costing thousands in closing costs that means turning over even more of your money to the bank.
2. Selling your home! Well, that's not a realistic option.

Even if you could live this way, it requires loads of discipline with very little flexibility for life events (medical bills, new car, blown transmission, etc.) Again, all of your savings would be tied up in a mortgage. That would be a scary 10 years!

Now that I have had time to experience and test this method, I am happy to announce that my research was right! It works! I started implementing this formula in December of 2013, and I will pay my home off in 16 months. I can also re-leverage my equity to buy assets--dividend-paying investments that further accelerate the payoff term. I can use the bank's money to make money!

So, I started to think about what my career was really doing to folks. I wasn't truly helping them if I kept this to myself. After all, I had become successful because my clients trusted me and because I cared about them first. It would go against the grain of my faith if I didn't share this.

I decided to start a consulting business, showing folks how to use this strategy with the same success I was having. Complete financial transformation!

The response has been nothing short of mind blowing. It's not a difficult concept, and the tools have been available to us all for decades. But, it does take a lot of education to avoid falling into another banking pitfall.

Over the years, I have discovered further concepts that work with this strategy to accelerate the payoff timeline. Also, there are many different types of HELOCs available, and some must be avoided if you want to maximize the potential of this system. Having hundreds of thousands of dollars at my disposal forced me to research the best ways to utilize this asset to further my goal of financial independence. This time, I wasn't going to make the mistakes I'd made in the past.

Before, only my wife and I had suffered the consequences of those mistakes, but now we have young children. There are few motivators more powerful than caring for them and having the responsibility of ensuring their future.

My faith requires me to give and spreading the word of truth is very important to me. I want to share this with every homeowner or would-be homeowner on the planet. There is a better way! What if a fraction of America was doing this in 2007? We wouldn't have had the meltdown we faced. Those folks would not only own their homes free and clear, but their vacation and investment properties as well, creating massive net worth.

I hope that as you read this book, you will decide to join us in this movement and change the legacy of your family forever!

A word of warning, though. You will be faced with opposition from your banker or loan officer. Don't blame them. They don't know any better. I haven't gotten to them yet. You are my first priority.

CHAPTER 2
Proof You Are Being Ripped Off With Your Current Mortgage

I want to say up front that this is not a get rich quick program. In fact, it will take years. The exact timeline depends on your income and discipline, but it will be years sooner than you would pay off your current 15-30 year mortgage.

Does the image on the next page look familiar? What you're looking at is an amortization schedule for a traditional mortgage of $200,000.

As you can see, the first 12 payments barely decrease the principal balance, because you're predominantly paying interest. For the first 12 months, you'll invest $11,800.56 to bring down the balance by $3,371.73. Doesn't seem like a fair trade, does it?

DATE	PAYMENT	PRINCIPAL	INTEREST	TOTAL INTEREST	BALANCE
Mar. 2016	$983.88	$275.55	$708.33	$708.33	$199,724.45
April 2016	$983.88	$276.52	$707.36	$1,415.69	$199,447.93
May 2016	$983.88	$277.50	$706.38	$2,122.07	$199,170.43
June 2016	$983.88	$278.48	$705.40	$2,827.46	$198,891.95
July 2016	$983.88	$279.47	$704.41	$3,531.87	$198,612.47
Aug. 2016	$983.88	$280.46	$703.42	$4,235.29	$198,332.01
Sept. 2016	$983.88	$281.45	$702.43	$4,937.72	$198,050.56
Oct. 2016	$983.88	$282.45	$701.43	$5,639.15	$197,768.11
Nov. 2016	$983.88	$283.45	$700.43	$6,339.58	$197,484.66
Dec. 2016	$983.88	$284.45	$699.42	$7,039.00	$197,200.20
Jan. 2017	$983.88	$285.46	$698.42	$7,737.42	$196,914.74
Feb. 2017	$983.88	$286.47	$697.41	$8,434.82	$196,628.27

Who's really winning? To find the answer to that, follow the money.

SEGREGATION OF INCOME

Before we move forward, you need to first understand a basic banking principle called "segregation of income". Banks want your money as segregated as possible. They want your money to be funneled down various rabbit holes like checking accounts, savings, CD's, and money market accounts. If your money is split up, you cannot utilize 100% of it toward a common goal.

$250,000	30 Years	15 Year
Payment	$1,266.71	$1,912.4
Interest Paid	$206,016.78	$94,246.9
Total Paid	$456,016.78	$344,246.

To ensure that your money is segregated, the banks advertise and offer traditional closed-end mortgages. Money can only go in and only comes out if you refinance or sell. Basically, your money is trapped! It would be financial suicide to put 100% of your income into a mortgage, because you would have nothing left available for living expenses. So, this forces you to put only a percentage of your wages towards your mortgage. It doesn't matter if it's a big percentage or a small percentage. At the end of the day, it's still just a percentage. That means you stay in debt longer. The longer you stay in debt, the more interest you pay and the more profit the bank makes. This is common knowledge.

But what about the portion you left sitting in a checking account waiting to be spent? Well, that's the other money maker. Banks leverage your depository accounts to manifest "electronic money" out of thin air. They are lending your money out the back door for higher-yielding investments and loans to consumers...including you! That's right. You are probably borrowing your own money back from the bank at a much higher rate. So, mortgages are just one of the ways banks make money off of your transfer of wealth. They are very much after your checking accounts as well.

This is another reason a HELOC is the perfect tool. It merges two financial products, a mortgage and a checking account, without losing liquidity.

What you're looking at here is a $250,000 traditional mortgage product at 4.5%. Over the course of 30 years, you'll have paid $456,016.78. Although right now we're in a great real estate market where homes are appreciating at 2-4%, you have to ask yourself, "At what rate will my home have to appreciate for me to get back the money that I spent?" It will probably never be worth that much, and although a 15 year program is far better than a 30 year program, you're still paying $94,246.98 in interest. That may sound like a lot, and it is compared to a proper HELOC strategy.

$250,000	30 Years	15 Years
Payment	$1,266.71	$1,912.48
Interest Paid	$206,016.78	$94,246.98
Total Paid	$456,016.78	$344,246.98

Again, you're still going to pay far more than your home will be worth, maybe ever. If you're paying mortgage insurance on top of that, you're going to further inflate the cost. Basically you don't own your home. You're just renting from the bank. If that didn't make you sick to your stomach, let's talk about closing costs on top of the amount of interest that you'll pay.

What you're looking at here below is a graph showing the average mortgage closing costs by state in 2014. Some states are higher than others, so let's talk about the national average. The United States national average for closing costs is $2,525 That is based on a $200,000 loan with 20% down and a good FICO score.

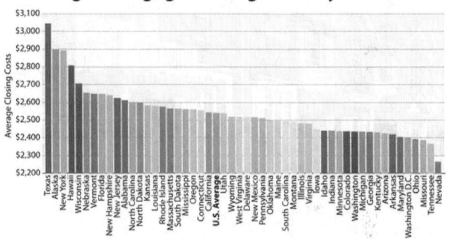

Average Mortgage Closing Costs By State, 2014

Data: Bankrate.com; $200k loan, 20% down, good FICO   ©ChartForce Do not reproduce without permission.

If you have less than perfect credit and you're putting less money down, your cost probably will be much higher than this $2,525 figure. Where does that closing cost come from? That's underwriting fees, processing fees, application fees, credit report fees, origination points, and discount points. In our industry we call these junk fees. The reason they're called junk fees? It's additional profit generated without providing any additional benefit to the borrower.

Don't be confused by some of those programs out there like the "no closing cost mortgage". What the bank is really doing is marking up the interest rate in order to pay those closing costs on your behalf. If it weren't for that "no closing costs" deal, you would qualify for a lower interest rate and a lower payment over a longer period of time.

See, the bank is going to make money one way or the other. They're either going to make it on the interest rate side, or they're going to make it on the closing cost side. Either way, the bank is making its money with your money.

I know we've already touched on mortgage insurance, but I want to go into further detail. As you can already imagine, the mortgage insurance requirement truly disgusts me. You'll see why in a moment, but let's start with the basics. Mortgage insurance is something that is required by the bank or lender if you're buying and putting less than 20% down, or if you're refinancing and you have less than 20% equity based on the appraisal. Really, it's just a slush fund that goes to a mortgage insurance company and protects the bank in case you default.

Now, let's talk about the different programs that have various forms of mortgage insurance, FHA being one. FHA charges 1.75% up front. That is on top of your loan amount. For example, if you're taking out a $100,000 loan, you're actually going to finance $101,750 instead of that $100,000. That's going to increase your loan amount, which will in turn raise the amount of interest you pay.

In addition, they're going to charge 85 basis points monthly. You're going to have a higher payment per month than you normally would with FHA.

With VA, they charge up to 3.3%. VA calls it a funding fee, but it's essentially the same thing, just different terminology. For example, if you take out a $200,000 loan, you're really going to finance $206,600, because you're going to have a $6,600 funding fee going to VA in case you default. I had a recent client who had a $400,000 VA loan and paid over $13,000 in a funding fee that was financed on top of his loan.

USDA is another program that offers 100% financing, very similar to VA, and it's limited based on area and income. They charge 2.75% up front, and they call this a guarantee fee. Again different terminology, but essentially it's just mortgage insurance that goes to USDA. On top of that 2.75% up front, they also charge 50 basis points monthly.

Conventional mortgage lenders can sometimes be more aggressive and sometimes cheaper. As you can see here, you can pay as little as 0.27% monthly -that's usually for folks who have excellent credit and a lot of money to put down, but still less than 20%--and up to 1.48% of monthly private mortgage insurance (PMI). That tends to be your customers with lower credit scores that are putting 3-5% down.

Follow the Money: Compare MI Costs

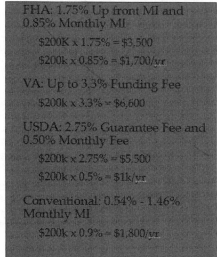

FHA: 1.75% Up front MI and 0.85% Monthly MI

$200K x 1.75% = $3,500

$200k x 0.85% = $1,700/yr

VA: Up to 3.3% Funding Fee

$200k x 3.3% = $6,600

USDA: 2.75% Guarantee Fee and 0.50% Monthly Fee

$200k x 2.75% = $5,500

$200k x 0.5% = $1k/yr

Conventional: 0.54% - 1.46% Monthly MI

$200k x 0.9% = $1,800/yr

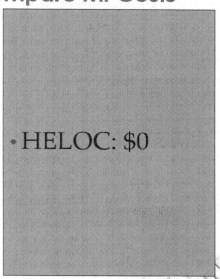

• HELOC: $0

Now, this has no benefit to you. Mortgage insurance is not mortgage protection insurance, it's an entirely different product.

There are some programs out there being advertised as 5% down with no mortgage insurance. This works just like the "no closing costs" deal described earlier. The bank is actually marking up your interest rate to absorb those costs. Let's say you qualified for a 4% interest rate. The bank offering "no mortgage insurance" is going to offer you a higher interest rate, such as 4.5%, and pay that mortgage insurance premium on your behalf.

This method is a little bit deceiving because you will see a lower payment on a monthly basis, but you're financing all of that debt at a higher interest rate. Over the lifetime of that loan, you'll end up paying thousands of dollars more. You could have just opted for the mortgage insurance in the short term and eventually that mortgage insurance would fall off, but you would also have the lower interest rate. Just like drugs and debt, just say "no" to mortgage insurance. There's no benefit to you. It's wasting thousands and thousands of dollars. A home equity line of credit never has mortgage insurance.

You're probably asking yourself, "If there's a better way, then why doesn't the bank tell me?"

The number one reason is that they don't want you to know. The more interest and closing costs you pay, the more they profit. Refer to your mortgage statement as an example. And, we're not just talking about the bank's profit, we're also talking about the banker's profit or the loan officer's profit.

A home equity line of credit just doesn't pay well. A home equity line of credit will pay a banker anywhere from nothing to as high as $750. You may be saying, "Well, $750 is not all that bad." Compare that to a traditional mortgage, though, where the banker or loan officer is going to make four to five times that amount. Long story short, a home equity line of credit just doesn't pay off like a traditional mortgage or refinance, and it doesn't provide incentive for the bank or a loan officer to give you the proper product.

The next reason is that most bankers and loan officers don't know much about the product. They don't understand this strategy. They are just like I was and they're institutionalized to think the only way to save you money is to either lower your rate by extending your term and lowering your payment or reduce your term by drastically increasing your mortgage payment.

In my own personal situation, I talked to at least nine or ten banks before choosing my home equity line of credit. Do you know how many of those bankers or loan officers understood what I was trying to achieve and the strategy I was going for? Zero. None. Because of my experience, I created quite the extensive list of vendors, banks, lenders, and credit unions that I recommend to clients for the best terms and products. I would speak to four or five different individuals at each bank or credit union and none of them understood the strategy. Luckily for me, some of them have become clients. If these folks don't understand the strategy, how are they going to inform you as the consumer?

Okay, so finally, on to the sexy part. This is my favorite part, which is the solution. We have to understand the problem in order to know where we're going, and we have to provide the solution to that problem. Here's what you're going to do: you're going to finance your new home or replace your existing mortgage using a home equity line of credit. You'll need a specific one, and I'll guide you in getting the proper HELOC.

CHAPTER 3
The Ultimate Guide to Using a Home Equity Line of Credit (HELOC) to Pay Off Your Home in Five to Seven Years

Next, you're going to change where your cash goes. No more giving the bank your money at 0% so they can turn around and lend it back to you at 4-5%. What you're going to do is you're going to dump all of your income into your home equity line of credit.

There is no reason to worry. Money can go in and out of a HELOC freely. Next, you're going to pay your bills out of your home equity line of credit just like you would using your checking or savings account.

When I mention giving the bank your money at 0%, look at the rate of return on your money invested in a checking or savings account, or even a money market account. With an average rate of return of 0.17%, you're virtually getting 0%. Stop giving it to them. Instead, take your money and put it into your home equity line of credit. That drives your balance down and reduces the amount of interest that you pay monthly. A home equity line of credit is basically an extension of your checking and savings account. You have access to it 24/7. You can pull money out at any time to pay bills or manage emergencies.

This is not a new concept. Back in 2008, an article called "Mortgage Payoff on Steroids" appeared in the Los Angeles Times. Here's a quote from the article:

> "I didn't believe it at first," Bert said. "As long as you're making more money than you're spending, it will work. The accelerated mortgage system is relatively new to the United States, but it's been widely used overseas for years. In Australia, it's estimated that more than one third of all homeowners use such a system, and in Britain about a quarter of homeowners are said to use this approach. Now that we're seven years along obviously those numbers have grown exponentially."

This has been talked about widely on TV amongst various professionals. Fox News, Good Money, ABC News, and CNBC all talk about the benefits of using a home equity line of credit to accelerate your mortgage.

Businesses and corporations have been using lines of credit to build empires for decades. In fact, I have a good friend who is a chiropractor, and when he opened up his office he had to take out a large business line of credit. When I told him what I was doing for homeowners, he was very surprised. He said, "I cannot believe that you've been doing this for homeowners. I've actually been doing it myself." I thought he was doing it on his house. He said, "No, actually I've got a traditional mortgage on my house, but the same method that you're talking about I use for my business line of credit. That's what the bank told me to do with a business line of credit to pay it off extremely fast."

The reason is that it's the cheapest way to borrow money. When a business uses this same method, what they're using is a sweep account. It's the fastest way to pay off debt by funneling revenue back into the line of credit. He was able to pay off his business line of credit in under two years. When I explained to him that you could use the exact same tool to pay off your home, he was amazed.

Let's take a look at a real live example, just to give you an idea of the true math behind this and the power of using a home equity line of credit.

We'll use a $350,000 starting loan amount with an interest rate of 4.25%. Right now, prime is 3.5%. You can get home equity lines of credit well into the 3's. Obviously home equity lines of credit are amortized over a 30 year term, but let's look at the household income. This is $7,000, now keep in mind this is net, $7,250. Really, the gross income would probably be in the neighborhood of $10,000. Let's say this couple, a husband and wife, each nets $3,500 per month from a gross salary of $60,000 per year. It's a normal household with two working spouses. We'll also consider they have an additional $3,000 in expenses outside of their housing expense (groceries, cars, utilities, vacations, etc.). They get a tax refund of $3,000 each year, or an additional $250 per month average. What would you do if you had a checking and savings account? When you get a tax refund, it goes into the bank, right?

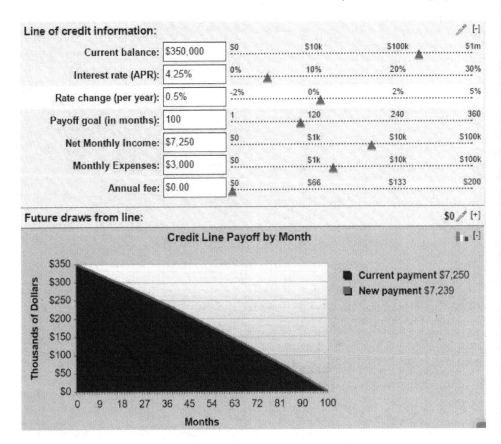

We're no longer going to do that. We're going to dump it into the home equity line of credit. Look at how long it takes to pay off a $350,000 mortgage with net income of $7,000. It takes only 8.58 years, without changing your lifestyle or expenditures! The total interest that you're paying is only $87,496 versus $200,928 of interest on a traditional mortgage. The interest that you're saving is $218,059.

Let's take a look at a more conservative approach, because you're probably saying, "Well Michael, we don't make $120,000 a year." Let's do the math based on a household income of $3,500 per month.

This is the net income that's hitting your home equity line of credit, or what would normally hit your checking and savings account. That's a household income of about $60,000, maybe $50,000 depending on your dependents and your tax bracket. I've lowered the loan amount from $350,000 to $250,000, because if you had net income of $3,500, you wouldn't go out and buy a $350,000 house. We'll use the same interest rate, and a tax refund of $3,000. With a net income of $3,750, you are paying your home equity line of credit off in 147 months, which is 12.25 years. You're only going to pay $75,662.33 in interest, which will save you $130,353.27. Keep in mind, I am also assuming that you are using a variable rate HELOC that could increase 0.5% every single year!

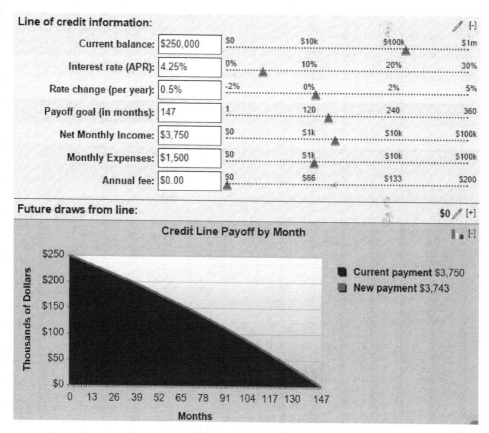

I'm going to show you another example with $4,500 in net income, and we're going to have a little fun with it. Let's say you get a new car every year for the first 3 years. When I say a new car, I mean a $15,000 car. New cars may go for $60-70,000, depending on your taste. But, if you have an income of $4,500 per month, you shouldn't be buying a $60,000 car.

Once again, we'll use a $250,000 loan amount, this time with $4,500 net income and a new $15,000 car every single year for 3 years in a row. Or, maybe it's not a new car. Maybe it's a life event, and you have such bad luck that it happens 3 years in a row and costs you $15,000 each time. Again, we've got the tax refund in here. Although you've had a major life event 3 times in a row, which is unlikely, it only increased your payoff timeline by a little bit. Now you're at 133 months, or 11 years, still only paying $68,000 in interest. Compared to a traditional mortgage, you're still saving $138,000 in interest.

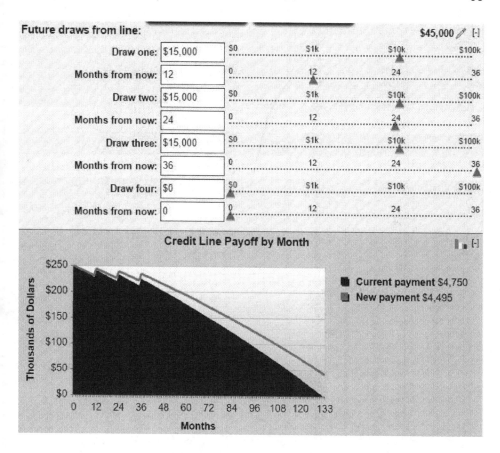

Here's a really cool concept to keep in mind, because we do know that unexpected life events happen. Medical issues arise, or just things that can set you back a little bit. With a home equity line of credit, those unexpected events are just minor bumps in the road. (Since we're on that topic, don't buy a car every year, and try not to have a run of bad luck.)

In this scenario, I'm going to show you a simple example to illustrate how a home equity line of credit works. It's a little bit more complicated than this, but I just really want to break it down in simplest terms to make the concept clear.

Let's say you start out with a balance of $200,000 on your mortgage. On a home equity line of credit, your payment is only going to be $698, but you're not making that payment. Again, you're treating it like it's a checking and savings account. You've got $7,000 of net income that goes into your HELOC. Your balance drops to $193,000, but you pay $4,000 in expenses from the line of credit, bringing your new monthly payment to $688.

In month two, let's say now you have expenses of $4,000, which is your home equity line of credit payment, your car, utilities, funds, etc. You've got a lot of expenses, $4,000 worth of expenses, more than you should have. Again, we're not looking at the best case scenario, but being realistic. The balance is $197,000. You have another month of income, put that $7,000 back into the HELOC, and the principal balance drops to $194,000. Your new payment is $677.

	Month 1			Month 2	
	Balance	Payment		Balance	Payment
	$200,000	$698.63		$197,000	$688.15
Income	$ (7,000)		Income	($7,000)	
Expenses	$ 4,000		Expenses	$4,000	
	$197,000	$688.15		$194,000	$677.67

This shows the impact in just a two month time period. You're going from $200,000 to $194,000 in just two months. With a home equity line of credit, as your principal decreases, so does your minimum payment. It went from $698 to $677 in just 60 days. That difference in payment is now going directly towards principal.

Here's something that's really cool about a home equity line of credit. Interest rate really doesn't matter. Interest rate only dictates what your payment is that day, not how much interest you actually pay. How quickly or slowly you pay it off dictates the total interest you pay on a home equity line of credit. This is much different than a traditional mortgage.

With this scenario, let's say you start off with a 4.25% interest rate and the feds talk about increasing interest rates. I think they will, but that it will be an extremely slow and moderate increase. I don't want to show you just the best case scenario, though, so let's say it explodes. For whatever crazy reason, the interest rate goes up a full percentage point every single year. That's completely unprecedented, but let's just hypothetically say the end of the world's coming and for whatever reason interest rates are skyrocketing. It's going to jump one full percentage point every single year.

Even if you have $4,000 of additional charges or expenses on a monthly basis, and $7,000 net going in, you're still paying the home off in 79 months. In seven years, you're going to get a $200,000 mortgage paid off, even in a rising interest rate environment. Interest rate is not the villain, balance is the villain. Something has to feed the interest rate.

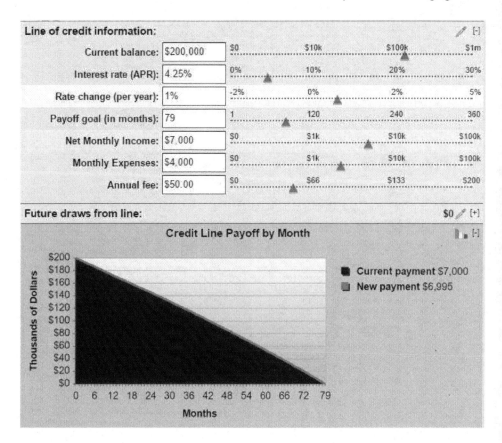

There's more good news! We've already touched on this, but a home equity line of credit usually does not have mortgage closing costs. Based on the national average, that's going to save you at least $2,525. A HELOC never has mortgage insurance. I've called around and spent weeks talking to different underwriters, bankers, and loan officers with different credit unions and lenders, and I have found dozens of banks that offer 100% financing on a refinance and up to 95% financing on a purchase.

If you're a mathematical critic out there you're probably saying, "Well, that's all good and great Michael, but what about a 10 year mortgage? Nothing can compare to a 10 year mortgage."

Let's look at that. Let's say you have a $250,000 mortgage, and this is a true mortgage. At a rate of 3.75%, the payment would be $2,501.53. It's going to take you 10 years to pay off that mortgage. But what if you did bi-weekly payments as well? That would shave off 11 months. You have no flexibility, so you can't get your money back unless you refinance or sell. The repayment period is still four months longer than a HELOC starting at 3.5% and increasing 0.5% every single year. A very low term fixed rate mortgage is a viable option IF you have the confidence and discipline to put every single available penny into your mortgage EVERY single month. However, you still have to use a checking account, where your expense money would sit waiting to pay your bills. That money is doing NOTHING for you in the meantime. It's just sitting there with no benefit.

I'm going to stop here and tell you about a friend of mine and recent client who works in an industry that has frequent layoffs. He does very well and makes about $135,000 per year. However, a couple of years ago he had six months when he was laid off and he was looking for a job. He said to me, "Well Michael, you know, what if I get a home equity line of credit and something happens and I get laid off again for another six months?" I told him, "Well, actually, being in a home equity line of credit would have saved you tons." Here's why.

He's going to start off with roughly a $350,000 mortgage. Based on his income, in about three years he'll have a balance of approximately $204,399. I said, "Let's say this happens in three years, and you get laid off for six months. You'll have a $204,399 balance, and your payment is going to be less than $700."

He replied, "Well that's great, I could easily afford a $700 payment." Obviously, if you only make the minimum payment, you're on a treadmill. You're not going anywhere. But, he doesn't have to refinance, he doesn't have to sell, he doesn't have to face foreclosure and he doesn't have to file bankruptcy. He has a very small minimum payment now, and just has to avoid falling into the bad habit of making minimum payments.

You can actually take this scenario a step further, because he's paid the line of credit down to $204,399. That means he has access to $145,000 of cash. If he wanted to, he could pull out $4,000 per month for living expenses and use a portion of that $4,000 to make his $700 HELOC payment. He could use the rest of the money to pay utilities, car loans, you name it.

Had the majority of folks done their real estate financing this way back in 2006 and 2007, we probably wouldn't have had the mortgage meltdown. Another issue with a 10 year mortgage is that it's still a traditional mortgage, so it's still going to carry additional expenses such as closing costs and mortgage insurance. Although a 10 year mortgage will get your home paid off in 10 years, you can see that it doesn't have nearly the benefits of a home equity line of credit.

Let's go into a bit more detail on a home equity line of credit.

Mortgage vs. HELOC

Using the home equity line of credit like your checking account will accelerate it even further, cutting the repayment period to, on average, five to seven years. You can't treat a mortgage like an operating account because it is closed ended. If you're accustomed to taking all of the money that you earn and depositing it into a checking account, then at the end of the month paying your bills out of your checking account, that's exactly what we're asking you to do with a home equity line of credit. Just use your home equity line of credit instead of a checking account. You're keeping your lifestyle the same, just changing where your cash goes.

I am a huge fan of Dave Ramsey's method of "beans and rice, rice and beans" combined with gazelle-like mentality, meaning you start a family budget and cut out the nonsense spending. If you combine this HELOC strategy with his methods, then wow...you'll be debt free FAST!

Advantages and Disadvantages

What are the advantages and disadvantages of having a home equity line of credit? First, a home equity line of credit offers a lot of flexibility. It has a very low payment, an interest only payment. That can also be a disadvantage, depending on how you treat it. If money were to get tight at the end of each month and a surprise came about, what you're required to make is going to be substantially lower than what a typical mortgage requires. But keep in mind that if you make that minimum payment on a regular basis, you're on a treadmill. You're not building equity. You're not getting closer to payoff. Be sure to use your HELOC like a checking account.

Second, it's open-ended with simple interest. It allows you to deposit 100% of your income with confidence that you can get that money back out any time you need it. What's left in your HELOC drives down the average daily principal balance, which drives down the amount of interest that you pay. Ultimately, it gets paid off much, much faster than a mortgage.

Third, a huge advantage with a home equity line of credit is that there are typically no closing costs. Banks usually don't charge any type of lender fees, and they will even compensate you for your title fees. It varies by state and the size of your loan, but if you're around the $100,000 to $500,000 loan amount, you can generally expect the bank to pay all of your fees rather than including them in the loan like typical mortgage lenders do. They'll actually pay it on your behalf. A lot of banks don't even require an interior appraisal, instead opting for an AVM (Automated Valuation Model) or Desktop Appraisal. And, there's never mortgage insurance with a home equity line of credit. It doesn't matter whether you're borrowing 85, 90, or 100% of the value of your home. A home equity line of credit never has mortgage insurance.

The disadvantages of having a home equity line of credit are really not with the product itself. It's really the person using the product who can create a disadvantage. What I'm talking about here is discipline.

What are you doing with your money now? You're putting all of your money into a checking account. All we're asking you to do is to replace your checking account with your home equity line of credit and you'll be just fine. It's discipline.

The disadvantage comes in when folks don't actually follow through on that. If you don't follow through on it, it's no better than having a mortgage. It's not worse, but it's no better.

Another disadvantage is that if you actually do perform the strategy, you're going to find that you're going to have access to a large amount of equity pretty fast. What are you going to do with that equity? Are you going to leave it there and continue to pay off your debts, or are you going to cash out to go buy an S-Class Mercedes? When you choose the Mercedes, you're buying a liability, not an asset. I only advocate pulling money out of your home equity line of credit to buy things that are assets. In fact, very specific assets, such as dividend paying assets--those that create additional monthly cash flow.

There is an additional perceived disadvantage of having a home equity line of credit in that the rates typically are variable, meaning they can change at any time and go up or down.

The reason I say that's a perceived disadvantage is that the impact depends on how you treat the home equity line of credit. If you treat it like it's your checking and savings account and you're cash flow positive, you're almost interest rate immune. What that means is, you're reducing the principal much faster than interest rates rise. Quite a few banks offer fixed rate home equity lines of credit, so if you're uncomfortable with a variable interest rate, it's easy to avoid.

Misconceptions

Let's talk about some very common misconceptions that I hear when I talk to clients on the phone. They'll call me up and say, "Michael, one thing that we didn't quite understand about the strategy is a home equity line of credit being a portion of the equity. We only have 10% equity in our home. How are we going to use that to pay off our existing mortgage?"

It's actually very simple.

A lot of folks don't realize that a home equity line of credit can be a first lien position loan. When I did mine two years ago, I only had 10% equity in my home. I called the bank and said, "Look, what I'm going to do is I'm going to refinance my existing mortgage into a home equity line of credit." You're not having two loans at the same time. You're substituting one for the other just like you would if you were to refinance your traditional mortgage.

Sometimes you don't need any equity at all. In fact, we found dozens of banks that do 100% financing. Ideally, we like folks to have a little bit of equity. We're not using that equity. The misconception comes from the name of the type of product that we're talking about, because it is called a home "equity" line of credit. In fact, that's where a lot of bankers get confused, too. They're thinking no differently than you are, because nobody's coached them or explained how this works. They're thinking that you can only use it in a second lien position, using the equity that's available above and beyond your mortgage. Nothing could be further from the truth. You can actually refinance your mortgage into a home equity line of credit that will be your only loan.

Mistakes

Let's address some of the most common mistakes that people make when using a home equity line of credit. First, you don't want to treat it like it's a separate loan, so that you continue to put money in a checking account. Don't just chalk that portion of your loan up as a different payment, segregate your money, and make a payment toward it.

The strategy requires that you use it like it's your checking account. All of your money goes into it.

Another mistake is not being aware of your weaknesses or limitations. In some cases, I interview a prospective client who lacks the necessary self-discipline to use this strategy. You don't want to use your home equity line of credit improperly. With most home equity lines of credit, when they give you a payment amount, that's going to be the interest only portion. That's why the payments are extremely small. Don't pay just that payment. Again, treat it like a checking account. Put all of your money into it, and don't worry. You can get your money back out. If you only make the minimum payment, you're not going to make any progress. If I feel I am speaking to someone who might do that, I turn them away as a client for their own benefit.

As I've mentioned, you're going to build equity extremely fast. Let's say you use the strategy and 12 months from now you've got $100,000 in equity and you've always wanted an S-Class Mercedes. Me, too! I think they're great to drive, but still a liability. If you swipe your card and get an S-Class Mercedes, it's going to depreciate 10% as you drive it off the lot, and 30% in the first year.

That is the exact wrong way to use a home equity line of credit. If we are going to pull money out, we're going to pull it out for investments, and very specific investments: investments that pay dividends and increase cash flow so that you can pay it off even faster.

Requirements

What are the requirements for getting a home equity line of credit? It's really not that different from getting a mortgage, but you do need to understand that a home equity line of credit is a bank product. It is a private product that the bank is going to keep on its books.

In contrast, 99.3% of all mortgages taken out in 2014 were government backed or insured. Any time you get a mortgage, that lender or bank has to satisfy the guidelines that the Federal Government passes down through Fannie Mae, Freddie Mac, FHA, VA, or USDA.

A home equity line of credit is what's called a Non-QM Loan. It is a bank loan, a private product for which the bank sets its own guidelines, policies, and qualifications. Usually, if you qualify for a mortgage, you will qualify for a home equity line of credit.

Some of these banks don't even have a minimum credit score. Instead, they're looking at the total health of the borrower's file.

Among those that do publish credit scores, we've seen requirements as low as 610 and as high as 700. To be honest with you, it's all over the board. It's kind of a double-edged sword. It's good because if you can't get qualified for a mortgage, there might be an opportunity for you to get qualified for a home equity line of credit. It's bad because there's no uniformity. I can't tell you across the board what it takes to qualify for a home equity line of credit, but you do need positive cash flow. You need decent credit. Sometimes, it helps to have about 10% equity.

Although there are quite a few banks out there that do 100% financing, we would recommend that you have at least 10% equity, because most banks go up to 90% loan to value.

BONUS

If you have 20% equity, a 700+ credit score and 10% in reserves, we found a special HELOC that provides several benefits that we haven't found in other HELOC's.

We recorded a video going over the actual loan and its benefits. If you would like to see the video, please send an email to michael@ replaceyourmortgage.com and we will send it to you.

Is a HELOC for You?

How do you know if a HELOC, or a home equity line of credit, is good for you? First off, let's take a look at guidelines and see what it would take to qualify for a home equity line of credit. What we prefer is that you have a credit score of 640 or above and no major financial setbacks in the past few years, such as bankruptcy or foreclosure.

Another thing we'd like to see is that you have 10% equity in your home. Granted, there are a plethora of banks out there that will go up to 100% financing, but having some equity is preferable.

Lastly, we want our clients to be cash flow positive. This is the most important factor when it comes to getting a home equity line of credit and using it appropriately. What that means is that you're bringing in more money than you spend. Take a look at your current checking account and see how much money is coming in and how much is going out. What's left over? Don't include the mortgage, but with the mortgage out of the equation, what's left over at the end of the month? The more you have left over, the more impact you're going to see from this strategy.

Another characteristic that we see in successful clients is a strong desire to explode through their debt. If you want to get somewhere fast, you're more likely to stick to the program and make the most of it. Our strategy allows you to pay your home off on average of five to seven years without breaking a sweat. It's not going to change anything about your lifestyle. If that strong motivation is a part of your personality, then this would be a good fit for you.

CHAPTER 4
The Top 10 Questions Everyone Asks

We conduct what we call free discovery calls with potential clients. During these calls, we crunch their numbers to see if this formula will work for them, and answer any questions that they have about HELOCs. Here are the top 10 questions we hear from prospective clients.

1. How do I take money out of my HELOC?
Many banks offer debit cards/checks/credit cards associated with your HELOC. You withdraw money like you would if it were your checking account.

2. How do I pay off my mortgage with little equity in my home?
Many banks offer 90-100% financing in first lien position. This means you can refinance your existing mortgage and replace it with a

home equity line of credit. This is not a loan on top of your existing mortgage. It is simply replacing your current mortgage just like you would in a traditional mortgage refinance.

Even if you cannot get a HELOC, we can show you how to perform our strategies with any open-ended line of credit, including a credit card. However, we recommend a HELOC above all other options.

3. What if rates rise or skyrocket?

Many banks offer rate lock options with a HELOC. In fact, if rates decrease, you can unlock your rate and capture a lower rate. Some banks offer you the option of doing this on three separate occasions-- yet another way a HELOC is more flexible than a traditional mortgage.

Many folks are rate immune when using our strategy. This means that folks reduce principal faster than interest rates increase. For example, paying 6% interest on a $100,000 balance results in less interest than paying 3.5% on a $300,000 balance. But, if you're concerned about interest rates, you have options. Many banks offer introductory interest rates of 0.99% to 1.99% for the first year. Just as with a credit card, you're free to go and get another HELOC with another introductory rate at the end of that year.

4. Can a bank accelerate or freeze my line of credit?

Yes, although it is very rare in a first lien position. Most freezes occurred on second lien positions where folks owed more on their home than it was worth. This put the second lien holder in a risky position because there was not sufficient equity to recoup its losses in the event of a default. A first lien position HELOC offers less risk to the bank than a second lien position, which is why most banks allow 1st lien position HELOCs. Our strategy will also give you positive equity the first month, and your equity position will greatly increase every month thereafter, thus reducing risk to the lender.

The bank can also freeze your line of credit for failure to make payments. This is no different than a traditional mortgage. In fact, a traditional mortgage typically has an "acceleration clause" that gives the bank the ability to call your loan due when necessary.

5. How is a HELOC different than a mortgage?

A HELOC is a simple interest open-ended line of credit. This means you only pay interest on the balance remaining at the end of each day. So, as your daily balance decreases, your interest on that balance decreases with it. Money can move in and out of a HELOC freely 24/7 during the "draw period". This gives you the ability to dump 100% of your income into a HELOC and still have access to the principal reduction at any time.

A mortgage is closed-ended and only allows money to go in and NOT to come out. A mortgage has a fixed payment for the life of the loan, based on an amortization schedule where the bank front loads interest. This gives the bank full control of the allocation of principal versus interest on each payment.

A HELOC has a variable payment, usually interest only. The payment decreases as the balance decreases. Every penny above the minimum payment will go toward the principal, much like a credit card.

6. What are the closing costs with a HELOC?

HELOCs have very low to no lender fees. Most banks will also cover your title expenses and appraisal fees when you get a HELOC, and will not add those costs onto the amount borrowed. A mortgage typically costs thousands in lender fees and title fees.

7. How long is a HELOC open-ended (draw period)?

Most HELOCs are open-ended for 10 years. However, there are some that are 15-30 years. This means you have the ability to move money in AND OUT at your convenience during the draw period.

After the draw period, the loan enters the repayment period, during which the balance remaining must be paid off over 10-20 years. Money cannot come out during the repayment period. However, you could refinance with another HELOC to start the draw period all over again.

8. What are the qualifications for getting a HELOC?

The qualifications for obtaining a HELOC are very similar to those for a mortgage. Equity, income, and credit scores play a huge role. A good rule of thumb is that if you qualify for a mortgage, you will qualify for a HELOC.

Unlike 99.3% of mortgages offered today, HELOCs are not government loans. Hence, each bank can set its own requirements for a customer qualifying for a HELOC.

Banks are typically more flexible with underwriting than Fannie Mae, Freddie Mac, FHA, USDA or VA. If you have an extremely low credit score (below 600), you may not qualify for the loan. You shouldn't, because typically your credit scores reflect your discipline or lack thereof. If you have an excellent credit score (above 700), you should qualify for the best rates and terms.

NOTE: We have compiled a list of 104 banks and credit unions, along with their individual guidelines. Contact us to learn which bank would fit your situation.

9. Can I deduct the interest on my taxes?

Yes, according to the IRS, you can deduct interest on your HELOC. Consult your CPA about how to deduct the interest. You will get a 1098 Mortgage Interest Statement at the end of each year from your lender, just like you do for a mortgage.

10. What am I paying for with your class?

We offer a class to further educate and walk you through the process. You are paying for a wealth of knowledge that will dramatically transform the way you finance debts/real estate forever. You will thoroughly understand the systemic methods used by banks to profit from your lack of knowledge and how to reverse the massive transfer of wealth from the bank back into your net worth.

We will show you how to effectively and efficiently use a simple home equity line of credit, credit card or any other open-ended, simple interest line of credit to capture any leakage of income that would otherwise be wasted on a traditional mortgage. Thus, you will understand how to utilize your income 24/7 to accelerate the payoff term in as little as five to seven years on your existing level of income.

Your lifestyle does not have to change! Just change where your cash flows. 90% of start-up businesses fail, but 90% of start-up franchises succeed because there are proven systems in place to insure profitability.

Our course is no different. We will unveil the secrets that wealthy individuals and businesses use to pay very little interest back to banks while leveraging the bank's money.

We will illustrate how you can use this simple financial tool to create wealth and quickly replace your existing income, giving your family financial freedom that few achieve. There are many varieties of lines of credit that can be used to replace your mortgage. You can use our cheat sheet to find out which banks/credit unions offer the best solution for your unique qualifications, allowing you to save time and thousands of dollars by getting the proper financial service.

You become a client for life, or until you reach your ultimate goals of being debt free and financially independent. Ongoing consultation is not only accepted, it is encouraged at no additional charge. You are investing a one-time fee that is a fraction of what you will save in a few short months of employing our strategy, and the results are guaranteed because it's mathematically impossible for this system not to work. If your loan doesn't go down much faster than your mortgage, we'll refund your payment.

CHAPTER 5
How to Vacation for Free by Buying a Vacation Home Using a HELOC

Let's say you wanted to buy a vacation home. You can buy a vacation home anywhere using a home equity line of credit if the home equity line of credit is tied to your primary residence. You can get a HELOC on a second home as well, and the financing options are more lenient on vacation homes than rental properties.

Suppose you wanted to buy a vacation home outside of the United States, and you've paid off a home equity line of credit that had a $350,000 limit. You could go buy a house in the Bahamas for $350,000 cash, because you're leveraging your primary residence which is back in the United States. Then, when you're not there, you can rent it out. The rental income will allow you to pay the home off faster, because it's being added to your already positive cash flow, increasing it and accelerating it. Again, all your income is going to go towards your home equity line of credit. Now, you're going to get paid to vacation in your home.

A more common situation involves buying a vacation home without leveraging your existing primary residence. Again, you can buy vacation homes using a HELOC. It does not have to be a mortgage. Let's use one of my favorite vacation spots as an example: Destin, Florida. Note, though, that all markets will be a little different. Be sure to consult with a local Realtor in any location you're considering to determine whether the financials will make sense in conjunction with your goals.

Let's use a three bedroom, three bath condo on the beach in Destin, a popular vacation destination for many folks living in middle Tennessee and elsewhere. In this market, you could easily spend $600-700,000 for a beachfront condo with loads of amenities. You will generally need a down payment of 20%, however we have found some banks requiring as little as 5%. As usual, we want to take a conservative approach, so we'll assume 20% down on a $700,000 property. That's $140,000.

If you don't have that much cash lying around, be sure to check the equity in your primary residence. After all, you should have your primary residence financed with a HELOC. If you don't have that much equity built up now, you will very soon if you're using this strategy. This will leave $560,000 financed on your Destin condo and a $1,956 interest-only payment. Property taxes, homeowner's insurance and Homeowner's Association dues will likely add another $1,000 per month, for a grand total of $2,956.

Here's where it gets cool! In Destin, these condos will rent out about 40-50 weeks out of the year. Winter months in Destin are usually November through February. Rental rates for these months are usually $300 per night. During holidays like the 4th of July, Christmas or Thanksgiving, the rates skyrocket to $900. In the summer, you could count on a minimum of $600 per night. Let's take a conservative approach and calculate on an average nightly rate of $500 and only booking 30 weeks out of the year. That's a total of $105,000 of yearly income or $8,750 per month. The other 22 weeks, you can go hang out in your own beach condo. Your HELOC payments add up to $35,472 for the year. That leaves $69,528, but don't forget that your property management company will charge you 10% to advertise and book your condo. It's worth it! Now, you are left with $62,576 per year of net rental income. Here is what your $560,000 HELOC would look like using someone else's money to pay it off:

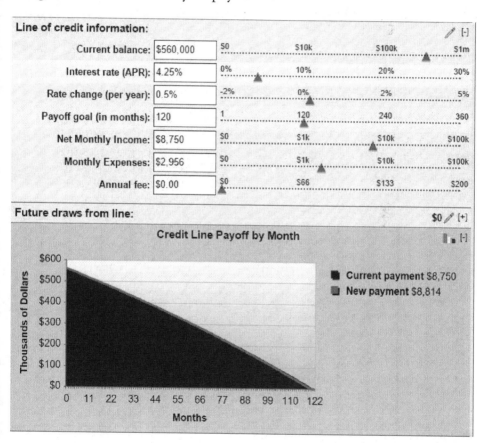

As you can see, your HELOC on the condo will get paid off in 122 months or just over 10 years. Want to know something crazy? That's if your rental rates never increase, which would not be a wise business decision! That is also using only 30 weeks of rental for a beach front condo in the heart of Destin, FL. What if it rented for 40-50 weeks? What if rates didn't increase 0.5% every single year? What if you chose a fixed rate HELOC instead? What if rates decreased? What if you actually used some of your own money? Also, in 10 years of 3% home value appreciation, the condo would be worth $940,000 instead of the $700,000 you bought it for. That's an increase of almost $1 million in net worth over 10 years!

So, there you have it, gang! Having that luxury vacation home is not just for the rich, it's for the educated and efficient. Stop putting off your dreams because you feel limited by assets. You are only limited in your thinking. Remove the filter applied by years of conditioned thinking. Do you think rich people only pay cash for things like this? Walt Disney borrowed money from his insurance policy to build Disneyland. Founder of McDonald's, Ray Kroc, borrowed money from his insurance policy to cover the salaries of his key employees during the startup phases. You see, the rich finance, too, in an effort to become more rich.

CHAPTER 6
How to Build a Real Estate Empire Using a HELOC

What many people don't know is that you can buy investment properties using HELOCs. We have a list of banks and credit unions that will lend on investment properties.

HELOCs are great for investment properties. Not only can you pay them off faster, but they have a low payment, which is great for rentals. This leaves you more cash flow positive than you would be if you had a mortgage on the property.

Let's use the example of buying an investment property. An investment property is essentially a rental property, a condo, or another home that's an investment for you. You may receive some type of rental income from it.

We'll use a $345,000 line of credit for our example. Let's say your net household income is $5,000. You go out and buy three properties at $115,000 each. All three of the properties combined are going to absorb the majority of your line of credit. You now have a $345,000 balance with three separate properties. You've got $4,500 of additional cash flow coming in from rental income. That's on top of your $5,000. As you can see, that's creating a residual $4,500 a month income in 5.4 years, because in 65 months you'll have everything paid off.

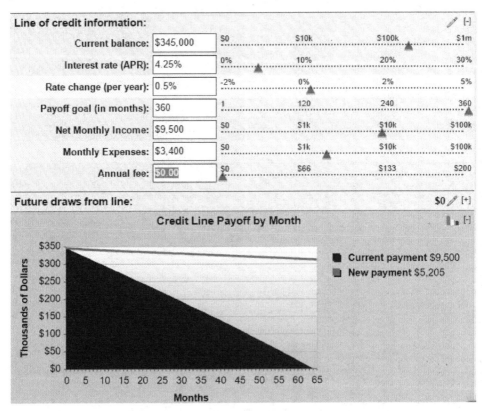

Having an investment property and rental income coming in on the same line of credit will allow you to pay it off much faster than was possible with your original line of credit, because now you have additional cash flow on top of your household income.

Buying flips is my personal favorite. I love the shows Fixer Upper, Property Brothers, and pretty much anything that comes on HGTV. Since the market has improved, flipping properties has become popular again. The issue with buying a flip is that when you go to a real estate auction, cash is king. If you have contingency financing, and you want to buy a foreclosure, or a bank owned property, you're likely to lose out to those offering cash. If you have a home equity line of credit and you have access to a lot of cash, you're essentially paying cash for these flips.

Here's an example. Let's say you buy a home for $35,000. I know every market is different, but in my market there are quite a few bank owned properties and foreclosures at $35,000. You invest $15,000 into it. I'm being conservative. You can go a lot lower than that, but I don't like to do the work myself. Let's say you invest $15,000 into repairs and you turn around and sell the property for $100,000. Now, you have a $50,000 profit, less real estate commissions.

If you do that four times a year, you've now created a $200,000 a year business. One thing I've learned about the mindset of a millionaire is that they love multiple streams of income. In fact, it's required. The average millionaire actually has seven streams of income. Using a home equity line of credit can provide a very neat and effective way to create multiple streams of income for yourself.

CHAPTER 7
Now What? What to do With What You Just Learned

We hope you have enjoyed this book. Whether or not we ever do business together, the information in this book can change your life and your family's life. So, now what? What do you do with this information?

You are more than welcome to keep doing what you are doing right now. We hope you don't though. We have equipped you with the right information and the power to change your situation. What we're doing here is no different than what most folks are doing outside of America. It's actually very common, and they look at the way we do real estate finance as archaic because it's taking us so long to pay off our homes.

In our course, we talk extensively about the pyramid of success. You have to start out with the right attitude if you want to change your life. You must have a success-oriented mindset. Although this is only the first step, it's the place where most people go wrong.

What I mean is that most consumers will refinance every three to five years when interest rates drop. Although it saves them money on a monthly basis, they're extending their term back to 30 years. Less than 15% of people actually pay their homes off in 30 years, and this is why. They're chasing interest rates. It's no different than what I did at an early age, and it's costing them tens of thousands, if not hundreds of thousands of dollars.

You need an action plan. All of this knowledge isn't enough. If you don't put the plan in place, you're not going to go anywhere. That's what we're here for. We'll hold you accountable and make sure you do act on this.

Even if you're not interested in leveraging your equity to build wealth and all you want to do is pay off your home in five to seven years, that's fine. This is the way to do it.

What you've seen here is just a fraction of the course that we've designed to walk you step by step through this process. You'll be our client until you reach your goals.

We are going to show you where to get the right product, how to structure it, and how to implement the cash flow strategy. Your alternative is to maintain the status quo, giving hundreds of thousands of dollars away to your bank.

I want to show you this graph just to illustrate the difference and disparity in mindset. In 1962, the top 1% of this nation had a net worth of $6 million. By 2009, it had more than doubled, to $14 million.

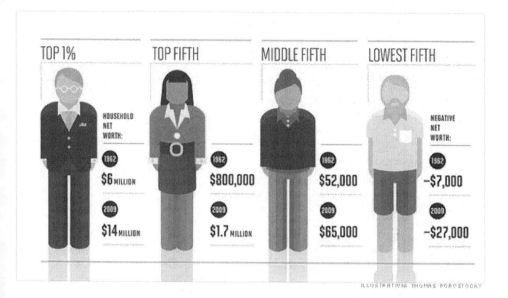

TOP 1%   TOP FIFTH   MIDDLE FIFTH   LOWEST FIFTH

HOUSEHOLD NET WORTH:

1962 $6 MILLION   **1962** $800,000   **1962** $52,000   **1962** –$7,000

NEGATIVE NET WORTH:

2009 $14 MILLION   **2009** $1.7 MILLION   **2009** $65,000   **2009** –$27,000

ILLUSTRATION: THOMAS POROSTOCKY

Look at the lowest fifth. In 1962, they had a negative net worth of $7,000. By 2009, they had a negative net worth of $27,000. They're actually going in the opposite direction, while the top 1% have made significant strides in the right direction. In the middle, you're not seeing a whole lot of advantage.

This goes back to having the proper mindset, with the proper knowledge and an action plan. We've heard it all before. The rich get richer and the poor get poorer. I want to add two keywords: "by design". You're going to determine which one you will be. Your transformation is truly our passion.

I mentioned our course earlier. Let me tell you exactly what it does for you, so you know whether it's right for you or not. If you're reading this book, you're obviously very serious about improving your finances. I want to take some time to acknowledge you for that. Most people never take the time to educate themselves the way that you just have. That's why you're perfect for this. It's specifically for people like you who want to improve your finances and decrease stress.

Just imagine being debt free and having the luxury of building a legacy for your family. I love this quotation, and it's so true: "Life is like a piano. What you get out of it depends on how you play it."

Let's talk about a few facts that you've picked up during the short time you've spent reading this book.

1. You now know that a traditional mortgage is a slow and painful way to pay off your debt.
2. You now know that this cash flow strategy is a simple mathematical strategy for rapidly paying off debts and beginning to build wealth.
3. You also now understand the importance of time and money. The best time to start saving money and investing is now. Time is one of the world's most valuable commodities. Once you spend it, you can't get it back.

Rich people buy time and poor people sell it. Make no mistake, this strategy is buying time. You're paying off debt extremely quickly in order to live your life doing the things that you truly want to do, not bound by your financial burdens. Are you trading hours for dollars? Or is your money working for you while you vacation?

Your goals are not going to accomplish themselves. Just like many others, I was a victim of procrastination. Not too long ago, I decided to take action. It has been nothing short of life changing.

I'm going to illustrate how debts truly dictate your life. There are 168 hours in a week, and at least 40 of those are spent working. Some work 50, 60, even 70 hours a week. I've heard stories of folks working 80 hours. I don't know how they accomplish it and still sleep, but they have to. That's the problem.

Let's just say you're working 40 hours a week. That leaves 128 hours in that week. The average person sleeps 8 hours per day or 56 hours per week. Now you're only left with 72 hours.

There's a cool graph on the next page, and it shows two distinct

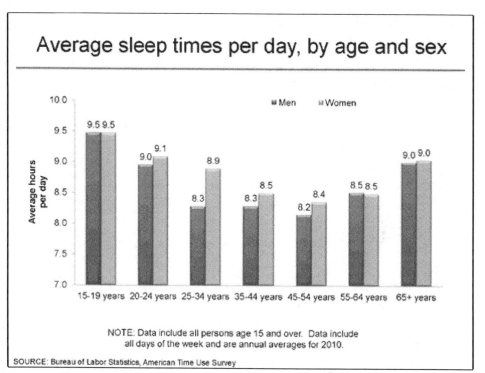

Average sleep times per day, by age and sex

NOTE: Data include all persons age 15 and over. Data include
all days of the week and are annual averages for 2010.

SOURCE: Bureau of Labor Statistics, American Time Use Survey

groups. One thing I noticed when I was reading this is the average sleep times per day by age and sex. Those 15-19 average nine and one-half hours, and ages 65 and up average over nine hours.

The 15-19 year old group is typically not working because they are in school. Not a whole lot of responsibility there. In the 65 and up group, they tend to be retired. Those who don't have to work all day and all night get more sleep and therefore probably have less stress.

The average commute to work is 26 minutes each way, depending on where you live. Obviously, if you're in Los Angeles or New York, it's probably much, much different. But, the national average is a 26 minute commute each way, or 4.33 hours per week.

That's only going to leave 67.6 hours in your week. I could continue, but you get my drift. More than 60% of your life is spent doing something that you don't want to be doing because you have to in order to service your debts.

This strategy gives everyone the opportunity to live the life that they want. It's not that hard; it just requires a little discipline and patience. It's really just set it and forget it and it's on autopilot.

You're not alone, because we are going to walk you step by step.

Here's a quick outline of our proven method to being debt free:

- You're going to understand the banking scam and how they keep your money.
- You're going to learn the difference between compound interest and simple interest.
- You're going to learn how to negotiate the best terms and get the right product.
- You're going to learn how to utilize a home equity line of credit even during an increasing interest rate environment.
- You're going to learn how to successfully apply the strategy, using additional techniques to speed up the process. There are actually a few more techniques that we use that can accelerate the mortgage process and get you to your goal much more quickly--maybe a couple of years sooner.

If this sounds like the solution for you, the next step is to book a free discovery call with us to analyze your personal situation. We are going to calculate your new debt free date based on using our strategy. Each person's situation and goals are entirely unique, so that is why we suggest a free call before anything else.

You can book a call at www.replaceyourmortgage.com/discover.

CHAPTER 8
5 Great Resources to Help you Get a Quick Start Towards Paying Your Home Off Early

Here are a few resources that will help you if you choose to pursue paying off your home in five to seven years using a HELOC.

- You are always welcome to call us with questions. Our 24/7 voicemail is 615-925-3887. We will always call you back during regular business hours.
- You can book a free discovery call so we can run your numbers by going to www.replaceyourmortgage.com/discover
- You can watch our educational videos as well as success stories at our YouTube channel. Visit www.replaceyourmortgage.com/youtube
- You can calculate how long it will take you to pay off your home using the RYM method by plugging your numbers into our free

calculator at www.replaceyourmortgage.com/calculator
* You can get more information on our course by visiting www.replaceyourmortgage.com/class

Bonus Chapters

CHAPTER 9
101 Ideas To Help You Make And Save More Money

As was mentioned in the other chapters of this book, the Replace Your Mortgage program involves living on a budget and the more cash flow positive you are, the quicker you will be able to pay off your home.

In this chapter we decided to include tips and ideas to help you increase your cash flow my making more money and saving more money. Some might not apply to you while others might be perfect for you. Use these tips as idea generators to help you reach your goal of being mortgage free faster.

1. Couch Surfing

Are you dreaming of traveling, but don't have the funds to go and do it? Consider Couch Surfing www.couchsurfing.com. You can register at the website to be a host or a traveler. It's free and an interesting way to meet new people. You simply camp on the host's couch for the night. Worried about safety? There are built in safety measures see the web page for details.

2. Car delivery

Now you are wondering how you can travel to your destination with little cash. If you have an excellent driving record and can pass a urine test, you could get a car delivery job. There are people who want their own car at their destination but can't or won't drive it there so they will pay you to do it. There are jobs delivering cars, RV's and even school buses. Who wouldn't love to go across country in a big yellow bus? www.carsdirect.com

3. Have you ever considered WOOF?

WOOF stands for World Wide Opportunities on Organic Farms. 45 different countries currently have WOOF farms. The assignments can be from a few days to a few months long, it depends on what you and your host agree on. You volunteer on the organic farm in exchange for a place to stay, food and a chance to learn about organic lifestyles. There are even some assignments that will accept you if you have children, wow, what a great learning experience for the kids. www. wwoof.net.

4. Volunteer vacation

Do you have experience in the medical field? Don't let the name of this group scare you off, Doctors Without Borders. No physician works entirely on their own. It takes a team of people. If you have had experience in any area of the medical world, consider taking a trip to volunteer in a third world country. The stories are heartwarming, the people in need, and you didn't really want to waste all that money on a resort anyway, did you?

5. *Get a national park pass*

The National Parks are beautiful and for $80 you can buy an annual pass that will get you into any park all year long. Better yet, if you are in 4th grade or the military you get a free pass! And here is a deal not to be passed up, if you are 62 years old 10 bucks will get you a lifetime pass to all the national parks! What a great birthday gift that would be! www.nps.gov.

6. *Rent instead of buying gear*

Now that you have your National Park pass, at some parks, you can rent hiking and camping gear. You don't have to own it, store it or lug it around with you. Simply go to the park, rent what you need and voila, you are on vacation.

7. *Get a state park pass*

Check out state park passes usparks.about.com. Buy a pass for a year and you can have unlimited access to your state parks. That's a lot of fun and entertainment for your dollars.

8. *Fly standby*

If you have some flexibility with your travel schedule you can do well with flights. You can fly standby which means you get a discounted flight if someone else doesn't show up for their reservation at the last minute. The flip side of this is flights are often overbooked and they will ask for passengers who are willing to take the next flight often the airlines will put you up in a hotel for the night, and the more desperate they get, the more generous the offers, often throwing in prepaid Visa cards.

9. Compare airline tickets with skyscanner

Give Skyscanner a try. They search and compare prices for 1200 airlines saving you not only money but time too! www.skyscanner.net.

10. Check out VRBO

With Vacation Rental by Owner, you can rent whatever and wherever your heart desires. An apartment, a cottage or a whole estate. Cheaper than a resort, do your own cooking and save even more. Obviously you can rent your place as well.

11. House exchange

Another way to keep expenses down and still travel is to do a housing exchange. You stay at their place and they stay at yours. Obviously some areas and situations maybe way more desirable than others. See www.homeexchange.com for details.

12. Refill travel bottles

Travel size personal care items are over the top expensive. Be frugal and refill the bottles and tubes instead of buying more.

13. Refill your water

The price of bottled water in airports is obscene! Instead of doling out money, carry an empty bottle through security and then refill, just saved yourself a couple of bucks. Tip from www.lifebuzz.com.

14. FOAP Pictures

Now that you are traveling join FOAP pictures. You can post photos from your cell phone here and sell them. This is truly passive income because your photos continue to earn you money while you sleep. The more you post, the more you sell. www.foap.com.

15. Odd jobs

There is a website called nextdoor.com which is like facebook but for neighborhoods. You can post in the group that you will do odd jobs for your fellow neighbors. Could be babysitting to handyman jobs. I know I have hired workers to help us around the house so I know there is a market.

16. Use Threadup for your fancy clothes

Ready to clean out a trendy closet? Sign on with Threadup www. thredup.com Threadup has a list of certain upscale brands that they will accept. They will send you packaging and postage all you do is fill the bag, send it off and wait for the check.

17. Have an eye for high-end brands? Use this tip to make money with Tradesy

Shop the donation centers like Salvation Army and Goodwill. These stores usually have 1 day a week that is half price. Find women's clothing that still has tags attached or is in very good shape and list it on Tradesy.

Brands like Pendleton, Banana Republic, and Coach sell best. Take a good photo and the site will walk you through posting details. When your item sells, they will send you shipping materials and postage. So all you do is put it in the package and send it off.

18. Drive others around

Have you considered Uber (uber.com) or Lyft (www.lyft.com) for a little extra dough? If you have a vehicle you can sign up to drive people around when it is convenient for you. Of course depending on where you live there maybe more demand. Think New York City versus Wamego, Kansas.

19. Pay yourself first

You deserve to be paid first and foremost. So decide how much you are going and let's get started. If you can set up a direct deposit from your paycheck into a bank, this is easiest. The money never touches your hands and is deposited directly into the bank. The important point here is to start. Even if it's only $10 a month, knowing you have some money set aside will inspire you to keep going and keep saving.

20. It's free money

All you have to do is take it. Does your employer have a retirement match? If so, make sure you are maximizing it. It's just like you have been given a raise. The percentage of what each employer offers for a match varies. Find out what your match is and get started! Check with your human resource department for details and sign up.

21. The days of paying full price are over

You can make this fun and challenge to yourself. How can I avoid paying full price? Shop sales watch for the weekly grocery store ads then go and stock up on the items on sale. Just make sure it is an item that you would normally buy.

Need "new" furniture? Think yard sales, consignment, and charity shops. You will pay a fraction of the retail price and find some really funky stuff at the same time.

The same goes for clothing. We live in a culture where the average person throws away over 700 pounds of clothing a year, most of it is not worn out, they have just become tired of it. You can find high-end brands with the tags still attached. To find these shops in your area, simply enter your zip code and the words consignment shop in any search engine and you will be on your way to an exciting experience.

22. Fire up the grill and cook your own meals

While we all enjoy a lunch or dinner out, a lot of money is spent at restaurants. Instead of eating at a restaurant, cook your own meals your grocery dollars will go further. Check http://www.foodnetwork.com/healthy/photos/budget-friendly-healthy-dinners.htm for low cost and healthy meals.

23. Shop the outer aisles

The healthiest and freshest foods are in the outer perimeter of the grocery store.
Any pre-packaged meals, mixes, or processed foods cost more and are less healthy which will cost you with bad health so learn to cook from scratch. You can make it fun, and your family will love it.

24. Beans, beans, the magical fruit.......learn to love 'em

Beans are healthy, delicious and full of fiber, plus they are one of the least expensive foods you can eat. Learn to love 'em and learn to cook them.

25. Meatless monday's

Make Monday's your vegetarian days. It's estimated you can save $520 per year by eliminating meat just one day a week. Best of all, it's healthy for you too.

26. Dig it! dig in and grow a garden

Grow some of your own food. It's a healthy and inexpensive way to obtain food. Do you live in a large urban area? Most communities have community garden sites find one in your neighborhood and start gardening.

27. Cook big

Now that you are cooking from scratch, cook big. Make a big batch of chili, soup, or casseroles use for a meal and portion out the rest in small containers that you can freeze and take for lunch. This site will get you started http://heavenlyhomemakers.com/meals-to-feed-to-a-large-crowd.

28. Brown bag it, or find a fun lunch pail

Grabbing a quick lunch out is an expensive habit and tends to not be very healthy. Make it part of your day to pack your lunch for tomorrow. Then all you have to do is open the refrigerator and pick it up and you are ready for the day.

29. Buy in bulk

Spices in little jars and cans are outrageously expensive. Find a store that carries bulk spices and you will save money. You can transfer the herbs into your own little jars if you like.

30. *Make a list and check it twice*

Never grocery shop without a list. A list will keep you focused, ensure that you buy what you need and keep you from impulse buying. Do what's most comfortable for you, write on the back of an old envelope, or on your phone but make sure you have a list before you enter the grocery store.

31. *Think generic, be generic*

Many people believe store brands or generic brands are inferior. Not so, give them a try. Often supplies come from the same place and just have different labels, with the same ingredients.

32. *Put your smartphone to work for you*

There are several apps available that will tell you when local produce is ripe, where it is and where you can get it for free! Check out https://fallingfruit.org or http://www.treehugger.com/green-food/have-you-ever-tried-urban-foraging-interactive-online-map-can-help.html

33. *Learn to preserve*

Canning, freezing or drying, are parts of our history, but sadly enough they are near extinction. Have fun and learn to do all three, then when you get free food, you will be able to preserve and enjoy it all year long. This site will get you started.

34. *Animal share*

Get your friends or family members to share a pig or cow with you.

If you buy directly from the farmer you will save middleman costs and purchase the meat at a much lower cost per pound.

35. Enjoy breakfast for dinner

Breakfast foods tend to be the least expensive foods consumed in a 24 hour period. So consider a second breakfast at least once a week. Think eggs in their many forms, waffles, pancakes, or cereal. You could even designate one evening meal a week as breakfast for dinner day.

36. Make friends with grains

Another healthy delicious food group that is relatively inexpensive are grains. Learn how to cook and use them liberally. The possibilities are unlimited and you will have fun experimenting with the many variations available.

37. Plan, plan, plan

The more menu planning you do the more you will save. It also makes life during the week easier because you already know what's for dinner.

38. Don't ignore the store rewards card

In the moment, it may seem easier not to sign up for a rewards card, and then carry it around with you. Don't be tempted to forgo this opportunity to save. Often you will not be able to purchase items at the sale price if you don't have a store rewards card.

39. Make this an annual new year's resolution

You may be thinking, "loose weight...again!" Nope, this one is to do a complete review of your insurance policies, renter, homeowner, car, life, health, and disability. Compare and shop around. The more you know about insurance and what your needs really are the more you will be able to save. Beware of friendly sales people who will try to sell you way more than you need.

40. Commit to the 30-day rule

Have something you really want to buy but you are feeling uneasy about spending the money? Make a note on your calendar and wait 30 days, if you still believe you need it after 30 then go ahead and buy it.

41. Get a library card

They are free and there is so much entertainment that you can get for free from the library. Beyond books, think DVD's, music, free internet, free programs for the kids and so much more, check the website for your local library's schedule.

42. Review and eliminate your club memberships

Companies want you to join their membership roles, and if you agree, they will take the money directly from your account every month. Review your bank statements and determine if there memberships that haven't been used since the turn of the century? End them immediately. Think gym, theater, and social clubs. It's easy to let it slide by thinking, "I'm going to get back into going to the gym." If you are not using it discontinue it.

43. Stop smoking

This seems like a no-brainer, but it needs to be said. If you are still smoking, stop. In the past 20 years, the price of a pack of cigarettes and the associated taxes have risen 343 percent. Let's face it none of us have money to burn.

44. *Go ride a bike or take public transportation*

While this is not feasible for everyone, consider using alternative modes of transportation to owning a car. Even driving an older car is estimated to cost $4400 per year, so if you can possibly get by without one, do so.

45. *Learn, learn, learn*

Read articles, books and websites listen to radio shows, podcasts watch TV shows or whatever media works best for you but stay focused on saving. If you get one new idea that you can put into practice then it has been time well spent. The more you know about saving the better you will be at it. Keep a positive spin on saving. Don't allow yourself to go down the path of, "oh this is no fun." Think of it as a challenge and allow yourself to become an expert at it.

46. *Become a host*

Become an Airbnb host or hostess. Wherever you live, someone wants to visit there. It's a great way to meet people and make some money too. It will take some extra work but hey, once you get it organized it's not that hard. Airbnb has safety steps built into the process you can rate your guests and they can rate you.

47. *Become a blogger*

Write a blog. Blogs are written and read for every talent that you could possibly have, be it blacksmithing, family life or quilting. If you like to write this may be very lucrative for you.

48. Sell your body

It's not what you are thinking! Companies sell plasma, and where do they get plasma from? They buy it from individuals just like you. Healthy adults can donate as frequently as twice a week, and expect to average $70/ a week.

49. Sell your expertise

Math, science, nursing, accounting whatever your specialty, there is someone looking for a tutor in that area. Connect with potential students at https://www.wyzant.com.

50. Rent a friend

Need a friend/be a friend. Is conversation easy for you? Started in Japan, Rent a Friend is entirely legal and becoming hugely popular. The website makes it clear that it is not a dating service, escort service or prostitution ring. Find out more at http://rentafriend.com

51. Make money caring for people

Find some extra work at https://www.care.com. You will find jobs from pet care, child care, elder care and much more here.

52. Start house sitting

You would make an excellent house sitter. People that can afford luxury vacations can afford to pay someone to stay in their homes, make sure that the pipes don't leak, the house is lived in and care for their pets. House sitting can be quite lucrative and can be for a weekend, semester or year. If you are really savvy you may be able to avoid paying rent for an extended house sitting situation.

53. Rent out space, not outerspace, just space

Is there a festival or large sporting event in your neighborhood? How about renting out a parking space. Have some clear space in your basement, garage or attic you could rent it out for storage. If you live in a college town think of students who don't want to move all their gear home every summer Think about the increase in mini-storage areas in the past decade and how you can capitalize on using your space.

54. Become a professional bridesmaid or groomsmen

This might not be a job for everyone, but there are some that really enjoy it. You could be a bridesmaid or groomsmen for rent. Occasionally, you will find a couple that would like an extra person to balance out the wedding party, help the bride with details or just give a little extra enthusiasm to the event.

If this fits your description, consider how you would market yourself and what boundaries you will set, and then get started. See https://www.yahoo.com/style/paid-bridesmaid-185027056.html

55. Sell information products online with a fire sale

Do you have a load of private label rights, resell rights, master resell rights or other content that you own the rights to just taking up space on your hard drive?

Then it's time to have a fire sale.Simply gather up all the content you have, make an unbelievably low, "no brainer" offer, and let your sale run for about one week. You'll make the most money if you advertise your sale on niche forums, via affiliates, via joint venture partners, on CraigsList.org and elsewhere.

56. Get $100... $200... $300... (SOLD!)

One of the easiest ways to make money online is by selling your "stuff" at the world's largest marketplace. Namely, eBay.com!

Chances are, you have items in and around your house right now that could easily bring in at least $100. These items include clothes, books, CDs, DVDs, toys, games, electronics, exercise equipment, antiques and so on.

Just be sure to take good pictures, write a descriptive eye-catching title and a good ad... and you're sure to get top dollar for your wares.

57. *Flipping virtual real estate*

If you have a few extra dollars to invest, then head over to eBay. com, SitePoint.com, DNForum.com, and DigitalPoint.com to see their website offerings. There you'll regularly find "under monetized" sites – those are sites with good content, decent traffic, but little if any profits.

Your mission (should you choose to accept it) is to snap up these under-performing websites, tweak them to make them more profitable, and then resell them. You can resell them on the same list of sites mentioned above.

If you don't have enough money to buy an existing website, no problem. You can also buy a domain (which is less than $10), purchase hosting (also less than $10), install a WordPress blog script, load it with niche content and resell it. It only takes a few hours to create, and you can be in profit just a few days later.

58. *Domaining – buy, flip and profit*

Revisit some of the forum marketplaces listed in the previous section, and you'll also see domain names for sale. You might be able to pick up a few good bargain names that you can flip in another marketplace for a profit.

Alternatively, you can hand register new domain names and immediately sell them for a profit on eBay, SitePoint.com or similar.

If you go this route, you'll need to study past sales to see what sorts of names are in demand. Usually, keyword rich names, names that capture a current trend (like "go green" names) or names that tap into a big news event tend to move fast.

59. Trash to cash

Back in idea #2, I mentioned that you could sell your stuff on eBay, including clothes, books, exercise equipment and more. Only problem is, eBay charges listing selling fees. If you want to sell your items fast and free, then check out CraigsList.org... especially if you're trying to sell big items that can't be shipped easily.

And if you're not selling large items? Then feel free to post your ads in more populous regions, which gives you a better chance of turning your trash into cash.

61. Do the CraigsList / eBay two step

Even though selling your possessions on eBay and CraigsList can bring you fast cash, eventually you'll run out of things to sell... and the money dries up.

The solution? Start selling other people's items. The quickest way to do that is by buying items on eBay and selling them on CraigsList, or vice versa. You can even place "want ads" on CraigsList for specific items that you know will sell well on eBay, negotiate with the seller for a low price, and flip them for a profit on eBay or other niche auctions or marketplaces. You can also use sites like USFreeads.com to buy or sell items.

Here's the key – sell what you know. And if you don't know much about an item, use eBay's "past auction" search feature to get an idea of how much your item will likely sell for. If you're not sure that you can make a profit, then don't buy it.

62. Get a little help from your friends

If you've spent any time in your chosen niche, then chances are you've developed a few friendships along the way. Perhaps you've networked on social media sites, commented on blogs, or developed a good reputation on niche forums. Whatever the case might be, now is the time for you to "cash in" on those friendships.

How? By asking your business associates, friends and acquaintances to join you in a joint venture.

In order to make money fast, you obviously need a product to make this work. You can create an information product (like an ebook, audio recording or video) fairly fast – in some cases, you may be able to create something in as little as a few hours or a day or two. Then you can write a sales letter, set up payment buttons and affiliate program through Clickbank.com, and ask your partners to promote immediately.

If you're unable to create the product yourself, you have two options…

One way is to outsource it to a competent freelancer. A second idea is to ask your JV partners to help you create the product. For example, you can conduct a teleseminar series with your partners serving as a panel of experts. Not only will you make money charging a fee to attend the live teleseminar, but you'll also have the recordings and transcripts to sell later as a product!

63. Turn your words into cash

If you can write, then there's a world of opportunity waiting for you. That's because almost every business needs a writer of some sort. After all, somebody needs to create the information products, write the blog posts, create the articles for content marketing, craft the sales letters and other marketing materials and so on.

To find work, use sites like upwork.com, elance.com and hiremymom.com to name a few.

64. Turn your talents into fast money

Even though good writers are in demand, providing good writing isn't the only way to turn a quick buck online. You can make money providing a whole host of services, such as graphic design, web design, programming, script installation and so on.

You can find people needing your services in the same places you'd find people needing writers, including Elance, Guru.com, Upwork.com and other freelancing boards.

65. Make Money... without a site, product or list

If your main assets are the relationships you've built up with other marketers in your niche, then you can make money – even if you don't have a web site, product or list.

How? By becoming a joint venture (JV) broker. Instead of contacting marketers to ask them to promote your products, you contact marketers to ask them to join other marketers affiliate programs. Then you take a cut of each sale (usually around 5% or even 10%).

Your job is to not only recruit affiliates and joint venture partners, but keep in contact with them prior to the product launch, keep them motivated, run affiliate contests and whatever else needs to be done to keep the affiliates happy and making money. In short, it's a pretty easy way to leverage your existing relationships to make money!

66. Consult your way to fast cash

Perhaps your area of expertise isn't in a school subject, but rather in a field that's of interest to businesses. For example, perhaps you know something about marketing, Internet marketing, advertising, productivity, employee motivations, accounting, cutting costs or similar.

If so, then turn this expertise in cold, hard consulting dollars. Set up a virtual shingle (a website) and let everyone know you're offering your expertise. You may advertise in the usual places (online or offline), or you may be able to find clients by cold calling, direct mail, or even dropping by the workplace for a personal visit.

Check out www.clarity.fm to sell your time.

67. Sit on a mock jury for money

Good lawyers want to be prepared for everything when they're handling a tough case. And one way to do that is by running mock trials with mock juries. These mock trials provide invaluable feedback to the attorney about how a real jury might react to their argument.

As you've already guessed, you can get paid to sit on these mock juries by visiting sites like ejury.com. No, you won't get rich doing it – but it's an easy (and interesting) way to pocket some fast cash.

68. Sell other people's digital products for fast cash

So far, we've talked about selling other people's physical products and selling your own digital products to raise cash. But here's yet another idea: You can raise money selling other people's digital products.

The quickest way to do this is by becoming an affiliate for a vendor in your niche. You can find affiliate programs by searching Clickbank.com or by running a search in Google (e.g., "weight loss ebook affiliate program").

The only problem is even though you might make the sales fast (especially if sell to your list, post on CraigsList, use PPC marketing or other quick methods), the payment may not hit your bank account for many weeks or even many months.

The solution? Find affiliate programs with same-day commission payments to your PayPal account, or find affiliate programs that pay

100% commissions directly into your account. Simply run a search for these sorts of programs in your niche using Google (e.g., "same day commission payouts" and similar terms).

69. Take pictures for cash

If you have your vacation photos sitting on your hard drive, then you may be sitting
on a gold mine! That's because there are people who want to use your photos on their websites – and they're willing to pay you for them!

One of the most obvious ways to turn your photos into cash is to sell your pictures on stock photo sites like istockphoto.com, stockxpert. com and bigstockphoto.com. If you're a fairly good photographer, then you may also offer exclusive photography to businesses needing certain types of photos. Search Elance and similar for these sorts of jobs, or post your own ads offering your services.

70. Trade Your way to a big bank account

If you know a lot about the stock market, AND if you have money to invest, AND if you are confident, decisive, patient and disciplined, then you may be able to pick up a few hundred (or few thousand) dollars fairly quickly by becoming a day trader.

This idea isn't for everyone. If you don't have the traits mentioned above, this method isn't for you. This is especially true if you don't know much about the stock market. If you need money fast – like yesterday – then now isn't the time to burn through your cash learning how day trading works.

71. Create and sell t-shirts and other products

Here's another way to raise some quick cash: Design and sell products like t-shirts, shorts, caps, tote bags, buttons, bumper stickers and a whole lot more using CafePress.com.

The bonus in using CafePress is that you can upload your designs or photos to CafePress and create your products right on the website. Then you can set up a storefront and start selling – with absolutely no out-of-pocket expense for you!

72. *Make money assisting others*

Earlier you discovered that you can make money offering very specific services such as writing, design, programming and the like. However, if you have a broader set of skills, then you can make money as a virtual assistant.

Virtual assistants perform a wide range of office administrative tasks, including but not limited to things like customer service, creating memos, writing the company newsletter, data entry, bookkeeping and the like.

If you have these skills, you can cash in on them by creating a website highlighting your skills and advertising this site on CraigsList and elsewhere. You may also want to "cold call," mail or personally visit businesses in your area to land a client's.

73. *Sell your possessions and products on consignment*

If you have certain items like antiques or perhaps even craft-type products you've created, you may be able to sell them on consignment through antique stores, "knick knack" stores and tourist destinations in your city.

Look through the phone book for these types of stores, then test a wide variety. Certain stores may take a larger commission, but they may also move your merchandise faster. As such, don't limit yourself to selling items in just one store.

74. Sell other people's possessions on consignment

If you know where to find buyers, then you can accept other people's products and possessions and sell them on consignment. Depending on what you're selling and how you're selling it, your consignment fees may generally be in the range of 10% to 20% commissions. So if you sell an item for $100, you keep $10 to $20 and give the rest of the profits to the product owner.

To find products to sell on consignment, you can place ads in your local newspaper, hang flyers, and ask for word-of-mouth referrals. To sell items, you may rent a weekly booth at a flea market, set up a small shop at your home (especially if you live in a busy area), place ads around town or similar. Naturally, you can also take these products and sell them online (eBay and CraigsList).

75. Take part in a paid research study

If you live near a university, there are probably opportunities for you to take part in psychological experiments and other paid research studies. But even if you don't live near a large university, there are generally opportunities to make money by taking part in other paid research studies, especially medical studies.

76. Raise money walking dogs

There are plenty of professional people who are unable to come home during the day to walk their dogs. You can fill this need by offering to walk their dogs for them.

77. Sell advertising specialties to local businesses

Ad specialties are those little "gifts" that businesses send to their customers, such as calendars and pens that include the business name and a small ad. Obviously, these businesses need to buy these products from someone – why not you?

To get started, search for "advertising specialties" in Google to find a variety of suppliers of both traditional items (like calendars) to unusual items (like beer mugs or Frisbees). Then approach local business owners and sell them on buying these items for both their customers as well as their clients. It only takes one large sale to put several hundred dollars in your pocket!

78. Sell internet marketing services to offline businesses

Here's an idea where you don't strictly make your money offline. However, this idea does require you to start offline – namely, by finding "brick and mortar" stores that don't yet have an online presence (or they're not fully utilizing the web).

If you know a little something about online marketing, then you can help these local businesses using one or more of the following ideas:

1. Create and manage a website for the business.
2. Optimize the site for the search engines (especially local search terms).
3. Set up tools such as blogs and autoresponders.
4. Manage the client's mailing list.

And so on. You may take your online marketing knowledge and skills for granted, but many offline business owners would be thrilled to have someone like yourself create and manage their online presence.

79. Do odd jobs for cash

Depending on the time of the year and where you live, there are always many types of odd jobs you can help people with, including mowing lawns, yard care, garden care, flower garden care, raking and removing leaves, cleaning up after a storm, snow removal and so on.

You may also do year-around jobs such as offering to clean out basements and garages, help people clean up in preparation for an estate sale, fix things like snowmobiles or lawn mowers and so on.

80. *Chop wood for cash*

If you're fortunate to own some wooded land, then you can make money by chopping and selling firewood for cash. You can sell it by hanging flyers in stores, restaurants and bars, by placing ads in the local newspaper, and by asking for referrals from friends and family.

In the winter, you can make large amounts of wood and sell it by the cord to people who have wood-burning fireplaces and furnaces. In the summer, you can sell small bundles (about an armload) for $5 or so by calling it "campfire wood." You may even ask busy places like bait shops and gas stations to sell your campfire wood on consignment.

If you live in the city, then obviously this idea isn't for you. However, you may be able to cash in on the next idea...

81. *Lease your prime parking spot*

If you own a prime parking spot in the city, then you may be able to lease it out. Examples include:

1. Prime parking spots near the downtown shopping areas.
2.
3. Prime parking spots near a college (especially if you can offer the spot for less than the fee the college charges for their parking spots).
4.
5. Prime parking spots near places like sports stadiums. Prime parking spots for special events.

For example, if you live on a busy parade route, you may lease parking spots and places to sit (e.g., in your yard) to people attending the parade or other festivities.

82. *Raise money renting out a room*

If you own your house, then you can raise quick cash by renting out a bedroom to people needing a place to stay.

You can rent out on a regular basis to college students or others who want to rent a place to stay for less than they'd paid for an apartment. Or if you're not interested in having people in your home all the time, then you may consider renting out the room during events in your city where hotels tend to fill up.

83. *Sell your hair for fast money*

If you have long, beautiful hair, then you can make money if you're willing to cut it all off and sell it to those who make wigs. Here are a few tips:

Don't bleach or dye your hair, nor use other chemicals to treat it. Those who buy hair prefer that it is as natural as possible. Take care of yourself by eating well and avoiding smoking, as doing so will ensure your hair is shinier and healthier (which fetches a higher price). You can search online for people who are willing to buy your hair, or you can post ads on places like Hairsellon.com.

84. *Save at Target*

If you like to shop at target, use the Cartwheel app to save on purchases.

85. *Walmart savings catcher*

If a competitor has a lower price on a product that you have purchased, Walmart will send you an egift card.

86. Save on gas

Use the gasbuddy app to help you find the cheapest prices on gas.

87. Save on hotels

Visit hoteltonight.com and get deals on last minute unfilled hotel rooms.

88. Get dessert

Instead of a going for dinner at a restaurant, just get dessert instead. Remember, it's the time you are spending with a person that is most important.

89. Save on babysitting

Consider taking turns babysitting for a friends kids and let them do the same for your kids. This way you can save money on hiring a babysitter.

90. Invite friends over

Instead of going out, bring people to you and everyone bring a dish to eat.

91. Clean out your closet

Captain obvious I know but this is a reminder that you could have some extra cash just sitting there in your closet.

92. Drink water

Some of you guys need to read this. If you have a Starbucks addiction or maybe you are drinking a ton of diet coke each day, switch it out for water and save money while getting healthy as well.

93. Change your thermostat

If you get a programmable thermostat, you can set it for different temperatures while you are home or away from home which will save you money.

94. Shop after the holidays

If you go a day or two after a holiday, you can save big for next year.

95. Volunteer

Instead of going out so much and spending a bunch of money, consider volunteering so you meet new people, help a great cause as well as save money.

96. Eat leftovers

Make a big batch of food and you will be good for a few days. This can also help you from stopping and getting a fast food meal.

97. Check the free events calendar

Check out the free events in your area and hang out there for entertainment.

98. Buy in bulk

There are staple items that you know you will purchase over and over. Buy them in bulk. Check out Amazon's service as well as local stores like Costco.

99. Downsize your home

Just because you can afford a bigger house, doesn't mean you should buy one. Really consider how you will live in the house and what rooms you will actually use.

100. Save on student loans

Some lenders will give borrowers a discount if they get setup on autopay. Ask your lender to find out what they offer.

101. Have a an emotional goal that fires you up

Focus on the end game of why you are trying to save money. If it is paying off your home faster, think about what would your life will be like if you were mortgage free. Having your goals close to you will help you be more aware of ways to make and save more money.

In closing, you just discovered 101 ideas on how you can make more money and save more money. However, a word of warning – just reading the ideas isn't going to get you anywhere.

That's because the key is that you need to take action on what you just learned. The sooner you take action, the sooner you'll begin to increase your cash flow!

CHAPTER 10
Rapid Credit Repair
A Conversation With Top Credit
Repair Expert Doc Compton

The conversation below is with Doc Compton (www.DocCompton.com) who, for the past fourteen years, has been helping people across the world repair their credit and save tens of thousands of dollars because of their increased scores. Enjoy the interview.

David: David Dutton here. I know some of our clients would love to get their credit score higher for obvious reasons. We're very fortunate because we've got Doc Compton here to do an interview and I'm going to grill him on credit repair. I don't know a ton about it to be honest with you, I know I'm going to learn a lot and hopefully you learn a lot. If you're in a situation where you want to bump your credit score up, feel free to reach out to him. He's one of the top experts in the world, he'll be glad to help you. Doc, thank you so much of joining us.

Doc: Absolutely, I'm very pleased to be here. I love to do good things for good people.

David: Let's talk about how you got into credit repair, please tell us about your background.

Doc: Well, like a lot of people in my industry, I actually needed credit repair. At the time that I needed it, which was right after I left college, there weren't a whole of people that were doing credit repair. Most of the people that did credit repair were attorneys and, of course, they charged an arm and a leg to do it. Obviously, being the guy with bad credit, I couldn't afford an arm and leg. I started just doing a little research and the more research I did, the more I learned and I started trying it a little bit, almost guinea-pigging myself, and it works brilliantly. Before long I was able to buy cars and get the apartment that I wanted. My friend would come to me and they say, "Doc, how did you end up doing that, because your credit was rats?"

David: Right.

Doc: "Oh yeah, I fixed."

"You fixed it. Can you do that?"

"Yeah, yeah you can."

"Can you do mine?"

"Well, I suppose for a nominal fee I can."

David: Right.

Doc: That's very much how I began the process. That's how I started learning. As much as anything else, it was just a question of digging into it and becoming a student of it, and everything from buying every kit I could get my hands on that they sold, all the office supply stores, books in the library. Of course, online wasn't really around at the time. I know I'm dating myself when I say that, but that's really how it all began. I was in retail banking and investments up until 2004 when I finally made the decision to go full time doing credit repair and it was the smartest thing I've ever done. I wish I had done it 5 years sooner, I'd probably be retired by now.

David: Well, you're really popular so I can imagine what your business is like. You've got a good reputation.

Doc: Well, you know as much as anything it's about longevity. I've been around for a long time and my industry is such that I'd be an idiot if I tried to deny the fact that a lot of people have come and gone in this industry. That's a product of the difficulty. There's essentially 3 classes of people in the industry. There's the people like me who've been doing it for a long time, who actually know what they're doing, they're compliant with all the laws and really do a good job for the consumers. That's one group.

The next group are the people that they try really hard. They have the best of intentions. They may not know everything. They certainly may not know as much as I do, but hey want to help consumers. They're not breaking laws intentionally and so on.

Then there's that final group and that final group are the guys with the cardboard signs that stick in busy intersections and on billboards and things like that because 9 times out of 10 it's an 800 number. There's no way to trace them. You have no idea who they are or wherever. More often than not when you hear a horror story about credit repair, it's usually sourced back to something along those lines.

David: To get to the obvious question, but, what is credit repair?

Doc: Credit repair essentially breaks down to the fact that there are federal laws and state laws too in place designed to protect you as a consumer. They're protecting you from having any kind of misinformation on your credit file. Obviously with your credit being so important all of the information that lenders would potentially look at to buy homes, cars, lines of credit, boats, RVs, you name it, that information has to be accurate because a large part of your financial future is dictated by how you look on paper.

They put in these rules to basically make certain that you weren't defamed in anyway by virtue of misinformation ending up on your credit file. It also established a mechanism for the average consumer to be able to dispute that information if it was found or suspected to be somehow inaccurate or incomplete, and gave them the opportunity to get that information corrected or deleted if it was altogether inaccurate.

David: That's cool. Does it cost anything as far as credit repair? What do you see in the industry?

Doc: It does. There's as many different pricing structures or billing structures as there are credit repair companies truthfully. Generally speaking the most important thing to remember is the fact that you cannot charge upfront fees for credit repair. For example, here in Texas, the Texas State law says that if you have a $10,000 bond and you're registered as a credit services organization with the State of Texas, the Secretary of State's office specifically, then you're allowed to charge upfront fees. The problem is the federal law that governs credit service organizations or credit repair organization, the Credit Repair Organizations Act, specifically says that under no circumstances are you allowed to take money or other valuable consideration before the services are fully complete.

Now, there's been court cases… there's been companies that have been completely shut down by the Federal Trade Commission and Department of Justice and different Attorney General Offices. I've always just defaulted to federal law because generally speaking it's going to trump. I've opted since 2006, I believe it was, to only charge fees after we've done some of the work. Now, there's some question as to: can you bill on a monthly basis? Yes you can, so long as you are billing for the work that's already been done. That's how we do it. We bill in arrears for the work that's already been done. Perhaps the biggest red flag when people are looking at any sort of credit repair company, regardless of what they tell you, they need to know that the federal law says they cannot charge anything upfront, no matter what clever name they give it, it's an audit fee, it's an evaluation, it's some fee.

David: They can't even get around it.

Doc: It doesn't matter. Every single way that some clever person could try to get around it's not an upfront fee. It's a something else fee, they've been busted for doing it.

David: Got you. Just for your service, for conversation sake, do you offer a money back guarantee? Can you?

Doc: Well, because we're a law firm we are held to a very high standard, that of course, being the State Bar, State Attorney General. We typically don't ever have to worry about it. I think anybody who's ever seen Tommy Boy, where the guy said:
"Well, it's got a guarantee right there on the box."
"Okay, I could take a dump in a box but it's a guaranteed box of crap."
       Well, my situation I don't really have to. I've never really had to worry about it. We do have mechanisms in place. I would much prefer to give someone their money back if for some reason they weren't satisfied, but the reality of it is very few people actually come into our system and leave dissatisfied.

       I've actually written articles, one in particular about my longevity in the industry is largely due to the fact that I'm not afraid to turn people away. I tell people all the time, look you're not a good candidate. For example, someone who is late on their car note 2 months ago, late on their mortgage last month and the month before that were late on a credit card. Well, that tells me they don't really have a credit problem, they've got a budget problem. The reality of it is if I start charging them for credit repair on a monthly basis I'm really only adding to a budget problem.

David: Right, right.

Doc: Let's say they're just barely floating by. They're maxed out on all their credits cards and so on but they're still making timely payments. I really have to have a difficult conversation with them and say, "Hey look, the fees that we're going to charge you, are those going to mess up your finances? Are we going to max out credit cards or are we going to keep you from being able to pay other bills, because that's obviously counterintuitive and counterproductive."
I'm not afraid to tell that person, as a matter of fact this morning, I had one that I turned away. She's late on a car note right now. I had another also today, my student loans are in default, what should I do? Well,

if they're in default, the first thing you need to do is either get them deferred or do a modification of some kind. Try to get them figured out, and start making payments on them ideally. If you can't make payments on them because it simply doesn't fit in the budget get them deferred.

David: Yeah.

Doc: Then at least it's not a rolling 120-150-180 days late every month, so you stop the bleeding. Then we can go in and start looking at some of these individual items on the credit and see if it's reported correctly. Student loans is one of the probably the most misreported or underreported perhaps, they're missing all kinds of payment information all time. Once those things are deferred we can really start to look at them and see if that payment history does make sense and very, very often it does not.

David: That's great. We do the same thing. I have a marketing company and do the same thing and then, of course, Replace Your Mortgage, we turn down people. We would love all the business we can get, but it's even right on our website, on one of the first pages, it says, "Is this for you?" If you're person above, let's have a discussion. Let's talk about it and you still may not become a client, but let's just have a discussion.

Michael turned down somebody the other day because it was too iffy. It's like we just do education, not the loan, but at the same time we, like you said, borderline, we're like look come back when you're more ideal. It's just the ethical thing to do.

Doc: Well, because going back to the longevity in the business, your credibility is everything. My name, my brand, my reputation in the industry is such that people from your industry reach out to me for advice. I'm not pitching people like I did back in 2004 when I was out knocking doors every day. That's just the product of people know that if I tell you, "This can be done." They know that I'm not making it up. Obviously I'm not a commission salesperson. I don't gain anything necessarily by fibbing to you about what can be done just so I get my commission.

That's one of the biggest problems I have with a lot of credit repair companies that do have the commission sales staff. I get it, sales makes sales. The reality of it is, a lot of these companies are charging $1,000 upfront or $1,500 upfront, plus a monthly payment for several months after that. Usually about a third to half of that upfront money is commission for the sales person.

I have people all the time say, "What's the difference between you and such and such company?"

"I'll say, "A couple of thousand dollars." That's my answer.

They say, "Okay, they must be good because they're charging all this."

I say, "Look ...

David: That's interesting psychology right there. They must be good but that's not always the case.

Doc: I hear all the time, those companies will very often say, "Well, you get what you pay for." A commissioned salesperson: yes, that's exactly what you paid for. If that's what you like and if you just really like that guy and you want to feed his kids, hey by all means. Knock yourself out.

David: Yeah. That's hilarious. All right, how long does this usually take? I know that's a broad question because it just depends on everybody's history and all that, but maybe an average of how long it takes to repair credit decently so maybe somebody can go get a mortgage or a HELOC in our case?

Doc: Obviously as you said, it's a loaded question because there's a number of different scenarios. Some people come to us with scores in the 300s...

David: 300s.

Doc: For those of you who don't feel that's possible, yes it is very possible.

David: I've never heard that.

Doc: I see them all the time. Obviously, somebody like that is not going to be done in 60 days. That's a little bit more of a project, because not only in that instance, that's someone who has been late on a bunch of stuff, they've had charge offs, collections, possibly foreclosures, bankruptcies, judgments, whatever it is. They probably don't have any good open, active credit right now. In that scenario we've got a number of things we're going to have to do for them.

David: Right.

Doc: Well, obviously that's the worst side of the spectrum. Now, on the other end of the spectrum, we may have a doctor, or a lawyer, or white collar executive, who's got a 735 and he comes to us and says, "Hey, I just need 5 more points because it changes my interest from 3.58% or whatever down to such and such," and they're buying a million dollar house. Even a very small fraction can mean a lot of money, and not only monthly but certainly over the lifetime a of 30 year or 20 year mortgage. Those guys don't take as long.

David: Right, just a few weeks.

Doc: That maybe something very, very quick.

David: Could it update in days, or is it 30 day increments, or maybe more?

Doc: It's a very dynamic system. Whenever the bureaus receive information from the furnisher meaning the creditors, the collections agencies, the individual jurisdictions where all the records are filed, it's when they issue that change, it's changed on the bureau.

David: Wow, okay.

Doc: Which means that if the mortgage lender is going to pull a report if they made that change yesterday the change to the score is going to reflect on that pull. It is a very dynamic thing. Now, everybody thinks, well they update on the 1st, that's not the case. It updates when that furnisher reports.

Now, there are some furnishers that will do it once a month, there are some that do it twice a month, there are some who do it once every so often, even though they're required technically to do it once a month. That's one of the ways that we go after a lot of these collections agencies, for example, as they report ... It was last reported 4 months ago. Yeah, that's not up to snuff.

It can be very, very quick. For example, I'll look at a credit report and people they say, "Well, how long will it take you to look at my credit report?" Well, me, it will take me 30 seconds to a minute to tell you if you're good candidate. You start trying to hold me down to timelines, and I'm really hesitant to do so but I can tell you I can look at this account, and this account, and this account. I can say these are ones that pretty much we'll have a 90% chance that we're going to have success with them. Then there's going to be that other end where it's going to be, "This is not going anywhere."

David: Right.

Doc: Now, people say, "Well, is it because it's a foreclosure? Or is it because it's a bankruptcy or this or that?" Really it's not. With public records, it's based on where they're filed. With collection agencies, even original creditors, it depends on who they are. I'm not going to give any of those companies the benefit of naming them, but there are companies that I look at and I'll tell the consumer, "Hey look, this is never going to go anywhere. Even if you pay it they're not going to do anything with it, they're not going to take it off. All they're going to do is show it as a zero balance. The impact of your score from that is zero."

David: Okay.

Doc: Then there's companies that I just happen to know that if you pay it they'll delete it. Well, I don't encourage that. They're not supposed to do it.

David: Wow!

Doc: Technically they're not supposed to do it. It's in their contracts with the credit bureaus that they're not supposed to do that. Keeping in mind that the Fair Credit Reporting Act was designed not only to protect consumers, but it was also designed to protect the integrity of the credit reporting system as a whole. If I'm a lender and I'm going to lend you money based on your credit report I need to know what the record is, what's the real record.

Let's say you've had 10 collection accounts, but just because you paid them all off, they were, "Okay, we'll get rid of them." Now you don't have that, well truthfully as the lender I'm not getting a fair representation of who this borrower potentially was. It's not to protect the consumer, it's also to protect the lending institutions, big banks and so on.

David: This is I feel like a loaded question, but can someone do it themselves?

Doc: Absolutely, absolutely. You can cut your own hair. You can mow your yard, change your oil. You can replace the transmission in your car. You can represent yourself in a murder trial. You can give yourself stitches, that a good one. The reality of it is if you let a profession do it the odds of success are going to be higher, the scar is going to be a lot less a lot of times. In some instances just based on pure efficiency it actually ends up being less expensive. Some of that is trade information and I can't really share why but it's true. People sending all this stuff out certified return signature request and before you know your postage bill really gets up there.

It's extremely time consuming. For us because this is what we do all day, every day and have for a really long time we're pretty automated and we have quite a system. Again, I can look at the report and know exactly how to dispute this particular account because I know it is wrong based on this particular minuscule piece of information. The average consumer is going to go, "I don't think this is mine." Well, the odds of my success on that one minuscule piece of information versus the consumer success I'm always going to come out better. Invariably.

David: Yeah, absolutely.

Doc: Yeah, you can do it. The laws are designed specifically for you to do it. Truthfully it is almost a little prohibited for people like us in credit repair industry to do it. There are certain laws that the creditors and collection agencies are actually exempted from in terms of getting sued if a credit repair company is the one that does the stuff.

David: Oh wow. Next one, should I pay off all the old debts?

Doc: My standard PC answer is that's between you and whoever you pray to at night, okay. Morally, yes you should, if you truly owe the money. The problem is, everybody quotes the statistics, some new, some old, about the number of American consumers with errors on their credit report.

I can tell you that '70-75%' average that's always thrown out there is actually pretty low, it's much higher than that. I guarantee you if you give me credit report I can find an error. Some of those errors are rather nominal, they can be personal information, they can be phone numbers, addresses and employment information, all those kinds of things, and I can explain why in a minute but there's errors. They're completely coated in errors.

Particularly collection accounts and the reason being when a collection agency is either assigned a debt to collect or they buy a particular debt to try and collect as the owner of that debt there's a transfer of information between the original creditor and the collection agency. Very rarely does enough information get transferred to completely validate a particular debt. They don't have the information necessary. I can't tell you how many times I talk to debt collectors where I say, "Okay, what was the date that this account first went delinquent with the original creditor?" They say, "Uh, I don't know. I don't have record of that." "Okay, understanding that that is the factor that determines how long it can stay on a person's credit report, what are the odds that you're reporting it correctly?"

David: Wow! That's really interesting.

Doc: Yeah, I mentioned a minute ago the personal information, names, addresses, telephone number, employers, this is especially true with Experian. They have a problem with what they call file merging. Let's say there's a John A. Smith and a John B. Smith, both of them born in Texas, which means their social security numbers are going to be similar, they both live in Dallas, let's say. Well, it's not at all uncommon for John A. and John B. to find each other's information and their credit reports. You say, "Okay, well that's problematic."

Yeah, it's especially problematic if John A. is a good guy who has $100,000 in available credit, always pays his bills on time and is a professional and very responsible with his finances and John B. however lives in his mom's basement and never pays a bill and so on. He ends up with an Amex on his credit report and John A. ends up with collections from John B from his credit report. It's important to maintain that personal information as well, it's not just about the collection accounts and so on.

David: Medical collections, do they matter?

Doc: They do. Now, obviously a lot of times depending on the lender they may not factor in medical collections, unless they're above a certain dollar value. They don't calculate those or they don't count them against the consumer as a collection and so on as opposed to saying apartment collections or a credit card that was charge off and sold to collections. From a credit scoring perspective they're no different than any other collection account, so they do matter.

I have a lot of potential buyers or borrowers come to me to and say, "Well, my lender told me I had a bunch of medical and it doesn't matter." Well, yes but you've got a 580 credit score and if we can get rid of some of this inaccurately reported medical debt then your score is now going to be a 620 or 640. Well now, you're right they don't matter. The reason they don't matter is because they're not there. It's not an underwriting decision, and as you no doubt are well aware if a person is at 680 a lot more doors are open for them than if they are at a 620.

David: All day, yeah. That's cool.

Doc: Alright, this is interesting, hopefully Dave Ramsey doesn't watch this, but should I have or use credit cards?

David: Absolutely.

Doc: Dave Ramsey is a smart guy.

David: Does a lot of good stuff.

Doc: He does a lot of good stuff and he passes along a tremendous amount of good information to people. I can't tell you how many people come to us, we go in, and we're wildly successful in their file, but they don't have any open active trade lines. Their score really just hovers at the 580-600-605, whatever. The minute they go out and get a secured credit card, for example, then all of a sudden their score is up to 640 within 2 months, just because of that, as long it's effectively managed. There's a lot of talk about, "Oh credit cards are the boogie man." I saw one that I thought was very clever, it may be Dave Ramsey that says plastic surgery with the cards and all that kind of stuff. It's smart until you need them.

Dave Ramsey doesn't have to worry about financing a vacation. He doesn't have to, he's cash rich and he's got millions in the bank I'm certain, I've never asked him. It's not a big deal. Now, if you're 22 and you've just come out of college and you've got a car that maybe your parents gave to you as a graduation present. Maybe it's on its last leg, you haven't taken care of it, and you're going to need a car. Well, because you haven't established credit you're not going to be able to finance a car through traditional means, which means that, "Okay, what does everybody do if they can't finance a car?" They go to the Note Lot, we tote the note, doesn't report to your credit. You get beaten to death on the rate.

Beat to death on the fact that is doesn't report to the bureaus. You spend all that extra money and there's no real benefit other than the car. Whereas if you're at a 620-640 maybe just because you've established a little bit of credit, used it effectively, managed it responsibly now you can go, and get a car and instead of a 17% interest rate, you're getting a 5% interest rate. Obviously, even Dave Ramsey would say, Suze Orman would say, if you take that difference in the monthly finance charge and you put it into even the most basic stock market based investment, into a college fund or retirement account, any number of things, you're going to come out a winner.

David: We've had the same thing, because obviously we have this cash flow strategy that we teach of putting all your expenses on the credit card so it pays down your income coming into your HELOC, interest is paid and, obviously we're in the same boat. We think as long you can manage it.

Doc: It's as simple as that, and I swear, this is a true story from today. I paid a whole bunch of bills last night, and when I pay them, and I pay everything online and I look at my cards to make sure that everything went through and check to see what's cleared and so on. I look at each one. Yeah, I've got credit. I've got credit cards in my wallet but I used them effectively.

I finance cars at 0%. My house is the lowest possible interest rate you can get. I'm okay with that as long as it's intelligent use of the money. I go online and I'm looking at this particular card and I was noticing that the available credit was like way more than I had any idea it was. I'm like what on earth? I go in there and I start looking and I go look at the last months' statement and I look at everything. Well, they just randomly doubled my line.

David: Oh wow!

Doc: Never even sent me anything, never told me anything about it, it was just this random thing. I'm not going to immediately go out and buy something on that card, but it's one of those things it's nice to know that I have. The other thing about that is, if you managed them effectively, keep the balances low, then your credit score is going to continue to go up. The cycle is either going to work against you consistently over and over and over again and push you down or as the case today, it's going to work in the other direction for you.

David: Yeah, that's cool. What's some of the best ways to build credit?

Doc: Well, I talked a minute ago about the secured credit cards. A lot of people know what they are, for those who don't essentially you're taking a cash deposit, you're giving it to the bank and then that bank is going to issue you a line of credit equal to that amount. For example, you go to the bank and you give them a $300 cash deposit or security, they're going to give you that credit card. It functions just like a regular credit card. It reports to the bureaus like a regular credit card. You can use it for all the things that you'd use a regular credit card, renting cars, buying groceries, buying gas, whatever. The difference being the credit card company is, they're covered, because they've already got your money. In the event that you ever default, they've already got their money covered.

The worst thing that they stand to lose is maybe late fees or termination fees, interest and whatever go up, but that's really a gimme, they're not out money, they're covered. That can be perhaps the fastest, the easiest way to establish credit. I highly, highly, highly recommend for people when your kid turns 18 get them a secured credit card, even if you don't let them use it. Buy their gas with it and pay it off every month consistently, build some credit for them, so that when they're 24-25 and they're looking at renting a place you can say, "No, no, no, how about buying one instead," and they've got their credit scores to do it and hopefully they're not burdened with too much school loan debt or any other credit card debt or whatever. They're able to get way ahead of the game about purchases.

David: We did that. We're big Dave Ramsey people. We still are, but again it's more balance for us now because I think a lot of his stuff is more general to the mainstream and that type of thing. We have just one secure credit card. Now we may be getting more or whatever. A lot of them are like low limit because you put what you want on it, but usually it's like $300 or $500 or something. Do you ever recommend putting say thousands, $1000, $2000, $5000, on a secured card and then having that or basically just keep building up so you can get a decent non-secured.

Doc: Well, yeah, either way. There's a couple of different ways and obviously the secured credit card is probably the most accessible way. Another way that people can do it is they can actually go to their own bank and either with a CD or a savings account, neither of which is going to pay much in the way of interest, that's the downside of low interest rates, you're not going to earn much on your money. At least you're earning something and it's readily accessible in theory. You can get a line of credit against either that CD or that savings account as well. Again, the upside there is you're earning interest on the money, if you give money to a secured credit card they're earning interest on the money.

David: Oh, right yeah.

Doc: That's a big disparity there. Now, even though it's not that much money, you got to win in the margins, I don't know if you've ever heard that phrase.

David: No.

Doc: It's David Bach that talks about that. Just every little bit on the outside, it's before you know it starts to pile up and that's a good example. Now, ideally if you manage that secured card well for 6 to 12 months before you know it, it's going to be really easy to get a regular credit card. Now, one of the downside, the interest rates typically on secured cards aren't that high.

David: Right.

Doc: For obvious reasons, they've already got their money.

David: Yeah, so it doesn't matter.

Doc: The annual fee on those cards can be anywhere from $29-$79 a year. Is it worth it? Well, it's a necessary evil, it's what you have to do to establish the credit so that you can do the things down the road. Once you've done that and you've moved to an account or at least have the eligibility for an account that is non-secured, typically they start you out with a $500 credit line, or maybe a $1,000 credit line or $2,000 or whatever.

I still tell people keep that secure card for another year or so just in case. Then when you're ready close that one and just use the regular one so that you're paying a lower fee. Now, you're still going to want to manage it responsibly, try not to carry big balances so you don't pay all the extra interest. Usually the annual fees are going to be pretty low depending on the type of card and the perks and benefits that come with it, but it's still going to be a better deal if only because you're going to access to whatever that security deposit was you gave on the secured card.

David:　　　Let's see, should I file bankruptcy or do credit repair? Again generally.

Doc:　　　It is but the reason we partnered in my case. I owned a credit repair company independent of the law firm for right at 10 years. For 7 of that 10 years, I referred a ton of business back and forth to Prevost and Shaff, who was the firm under which we now operate. We were sending over case after case after case where the debt collectors weren't playing by the rules, the credit bureaus weren't doing what they were supposed to do and so on. We were referring business over to them. Now, of course because they're a law firm, there's no kickbacks, there's no way for them to pay us or compensate us in anyway, but as W2 employees there's some different opportunities there.

David:　　　Oh yeah.

Doc:　　　Like profit sharing and so on. Some of the cases that we've sent over there are 7 figures cases. We're leaving a lot of money on the table. We finally made the decision in 2013 to bring it all under one roof.

David:　　　Smart.

Doc:　　　We operate under the same phone number, the same everything, the only thing that changed was the name on the door and of course the email, website and all that kind of stuff. The beauty of our current system is one of the attorneys Louis Shaff actually is a bankruptcy attorney and does bankruptcies. Obviously we have credit repair covered. Some people come to us and they've got $40,000 in credit card debt and I think I need credit repair. "Okay, what's making you ..."
"Well, I just got all this debt."
"Okay, do you have bad credit?"
"No, I'm not making any headway."

David:　　　Oh wow.

Doc:　　　$1,000 a month in credit card payments and just balances aren't going down and half of it or more is going to interest every month and so on. That's a bankruptcy client. That's not a credit repair. They just can't sleep at night because they can't pay all their bills. The credit repair client is someone who's gone through that, fought that battle and lost, had a bunch of stuff get charged off, they've got a bunch of accounts in collections, there's identify theft or any number of different things that have created all these errors and omissions on their credit reports.

Bankruptcy is designed to relieve people from debt, save the house, save the car, get rid of the revolving debt and gave them that tabula rosa, that clean slate, from which they can build for the future. Credit repair is really more of a, I don't want to say band aid, but its repair- it's fixing what's there from the past. There is some overlap sometimes but generally speaking they're 2 very different clients, the original profile. Whether they do a Chapter 7 versus Chapter 13, is largely depending on what kind of debt they have, what their income is and so on. At that point that's above my pay grade and I send them over to the attorneys and talk to the bankruptcy side.

David: Right. The biggest thing was the guy with the $40,000 debt, he can't really get ahead, and he's not sleeping at night, is that kind of determining factor type of thing when you're saying...

Doc: Yeah, it's not a question of if they've got a bunch of collections and a bunch of old stuff on their credit. This is "I'm drowning in debt".

David: Yeah.

Doc: That's the bankruptcy. Exactly. The credit repair guy is, look, I went through a hard time 4 years ago when my spouse died or there was an illness in the family. I lost a job and I was out of work for 9 months, those kinds of things and it was 3 or 4 years ago, stuff like that. There's a big medical calamity of some sort, that happens a lot. With the complicated system that medical billing and insurance works in, it is so common for medical collections in particular to be somehow inaccurate.

That's one of the things that when it made big news when I think it was a New York Attorney General sat down with the bureaus and several others involved, but they said we're going to change some of these things. Basically what they did was make the bureaus agree to really follow the guidelines that were already in place. There was a couple of other perks, not the least of which, was instead of doctors being able to turn over these unpaid accounts to collections in 60 days, it made them wait 6 months before they could turn over to collection.

David: Oh wow!

Doc: That's a huge thing because a lot of billing errors and things like that, obviously insurance companies can take 90 days-120 days-150 days to get certain claims paid. Well, by that time it's already been in collections and on your report and you're not even responsible for it. It happens all the time.

David: Wow that's cool. When Michael does these free discovery calls, which is basically our free consultation where we run their numbers. He gets about the same top 10 questions all the time and so we actually made our top 10 questions that we get because it's basically all the same. What are some of the top say 5 questions that just are constant for you?

Doc: Well, it's funny that you mentioned 5, because if you go to our website the page for credit repair has 5 tabs. What is credit repair? How does it work? How much does it cost? Can I see some examples of that work? Then online registration page. What we've done because we service people from all over the place, we wanted to make it as convenient and easy as possible even for that person who works the late shift and just wants the information in front of them. They can go to those tabs and read virtually the entire sales pitch. I hate to even call it a pitch because I guess on paper I'm a sales guy. The reality of it is: "Look I have the service, I've got this box with a big red bow on it, all you have to do is take that box, open it up. If you don't the box is still going to be here and it's going to be given to somebody else, but I want you have it." The biggest things are a lot of the questions that we've covered here.

Obviously, the cost is always a huge one. One of the most searched credit related phrases is "Does credit repair work?" I believe if you Google that now I want to say that we come up in there somewhere. Or my personal website comes up.

David: Nice, wow.

Doc: I have a pretty strong message for that and it's that I don't do testimonials. "Thank you Doc for helping me with my credit, I have a 740 now." Okay, "Ellen C. from Dallas." Okay, we all know, the joke is, you give me a 6-pack and an afternoon and I'll write you all the testimonials you want.

David: Right, exactly.

Doc: It's pretty much how everybody does it anyway.

David: Right.

Doc: We've never done that. What we do is we post examples, and when I say we post examples, we post recent examples and as of right now it was updated sometime last month, there are examples that are 3, 4, and 5 weeks old.

David: Yeah.

Doc: If you factor in that those people had to receive them, mail them to us, have them processed in our office, and then we scan them and redact all the data and then post these deletion letters, that's pretty recent.

David: Yeah.

Doc: There's a lot of companies out there that have up examples from 2008. It's like, "Aw, that's awesome."

David: Yeah. You're showing your game in 2008.

Doc: Pretty good for 7-10 years ago. What we try to do is show people this is what we're doing all day, every day for people right now. There's few things that are convincing or compelling to a prospective client them saying, "Okay, I've got this company, this company, and this company on my credit report." Then they go to our website and they go to the examples page and they go "There's that company and there's that company and there's that company," and they have a deletion letter from last month. I'm not going to guarantee you that we're going to be able to that for you but we've been successful at it as recently as 3 weeks ago, I would say that your odds are good.

David: Right.

Doc: We've literally had collection agencies call us and beg us to take them down because it was costing them business.

David: It was really cool, I'm a big believer in proof. We're a young company and it takes a while when people take our class and then they go apply for HELOC, 30 day closing, and a couple of months of doing the HELOC to actually see the results. I can't wait to start doing the proof of like This works. It worked the whole time. Before I called I looked at those letters and thought that's really cool you can't deny that.

Doc: The thing is, it's not just stuff from the bureaus, its stuff from individual creditors and collections agencies, original creditors, credit card companies that you know the names of, and I won't say them here because I don't want to give good press or bad press. If you go to that page and you look you'll recognize a lot of the names on that page and having success in getting it done. It comes down to the information has got to be 100% complete, 100 timely, accurate and verifiable. If it doesn't meet those standards either because it's in federal law or because it's industry standard then that information is subject to correction or deletion under those same federal laws and that's what opens the door for us to do what we do.

David: How long do bureaus give a consumer to where they are shopping around, how many lenders can pull their credit with it still being calculated as one pull, instead of say 40?

Doc: It depends on the scoring formula that's used. Some of the more recent scoring formulas will allow all of the mortgage inquiries within 45 days to count as one. The impact to your score if you did one every day for 45 days. If it's in the right scoring model, its one inquiry effectively. The score impact of that is up to or less than 5 points.

David: Right. Is 45 days, like United States wide or state by state?

Doc: It's based on the bureaus, it's not state by state or federal or whatever. It's just what the bureaus scoring formulas is. Which by the way, there's about 60 different scoring formulas.

David: Okay.

Doc: There's a relatively smaller number that are used by most lenders today, most of them are going to have between 15 and 45 days. The older the model, the more likely it is to be closer to that 15 day window, the middle 30 days and then, of course, the newest versions allow for 45 days. That's true of mortgage, student loans, and auto loans. The one exception typically though is credit cards. Every single credit card ding is a ding, every single time.

David: Okay.

Doc: If you go out and you go holiday shopping where they go to 5 stores and "Oh, would you like to save 10% on your purchase?"

David: Yeah sure.

Doc: "Sure, why not?" Then they're score tanks by 20-25 points just in that one weekend, plus they've got this new card with all this new balance, the score can tank even further than that. It's much better to have your 1 card, which for me is USAA, that's the big one with all the perks and cash back and all the miles and all the goodies. Put all your purchases on that one card, get all the perks from it, because you're not going to get perks from having a department store card.

David: Right.

Doc: Maybe that $10 off coupon or something like that.

David: Exactly.

Doc: Not like cash back and travel miles and so on.

David: Got you. Deleting collections accounts. Like it's not supposed to be done, it is done some, obviously that would help, getting it off your credit?

Doc: The thing about collections is there's essentially 2 things that we want to do in a credit repair process. The first option is always we want to update what's there to positive stats. Let's say for example you have a student loan that's 5 years old and somehow, somewhere there's this errant 30 day late in it somewhere. Well, if we can go back and correct that 30 day late, that's great because now you've got this 5 year old trade line with no late payments and so on. That's brilliant.

Well, too much emphasis is placed particularly by a lot of other companies on simply deleting an account. Well great, you deleted a 5 year old trade line, that's hardly ideal. What we really want to be able to do is update it, so that you get the benefit. Not only did you get rid of the negative part but you added something to the process that's a true win-win. Now with a collection account, there is no way to make a process. Paying it, and this is one of the biggest misconceptions out there, paying a collection account does not improve a consumer's credit score, not at all. I don't care what anybody tells you.

David: Wow!

Doc: I don't care what so and so lender says, I can show you on Experian's website where it says that it does not improve your credit score. All they're required to do is make it show a zero balance and there's really no impact. Now, that is maybe of some benefit to an underwriter's decision down the road, if you're right on that 640 line. But there's no balance on these old collections. Okay maybe we'll give you a break on this one. Other than that, from a scoring perspective there's absolutely no benefit to paying a collection, paying an old charged off account, again from a scoring perspective.

David: Right.

Doc: One advantage though is if you pay either a charged off credit card, or a collection account, the advantage is nobody can sue you or come after you. They can't sell that account to another third party trying to collect on it. Now, you've got the original creditor, then it's sold to a collection agency who gave up, and sold it to another collection agency, so effective you've got 3 derogatory or negative trade lines as a direct result of this one particular account. When you pay it, the one upside is that chain is not going to take place number 1 and number 2, none of the parties in that chain can then sue you for a balance that you no longer owe.

David: That's cool. Last question from me. Again, we may have already covered this, but quickest way and these are made up numbers, but quickest way to go from say a 630 to a 700 credit score? Secure credit card?

Doc: It depends on the situation because a lot of times you'll have people that have virtually no credit.

David: Okay.

Doc: If they have no credit well, yeah, I think that secured card is probably going to be helpful, but adding just a secured card is not really going to be the end-all. Simply because if you only have one card it doesn't represent a good mix of credit. The ideal situation is you've got a mortgage, you've got a car note, you've got 2-3 credit cards and all these things are paid on time. They haven't been opened recently and you've maintained them perfectly, that's a perfect scenario. It's very rare that you'll see someone who's 25 or 26 years old with an 800 credit score.

David: Right.

Doc: Largely because they simply haven't had time to establish the trade lines necessary to get what it takes to have that kind of a credit score, especially in those upper echelons like that. Again, going back to what I was saying about when your kid turns 18. Start it then, let them build some credit.

David: That's good.

Doc: The longer you're in the bureaus, the more likely you are to get to those top tier upper echelon types of scores.

David: All right, anything I should have asked you but didn't even know to ask you? Is there anything you think our listeners show know about?

Doc: This is one of my favorite tips and I've been teaching this for a really long time all around the country. I've been teaching it to consumers, I've been teaching to real estate professionals, mortgage people. Let's say for example you've got a credit card. It's the one credit card that you use consistently, say it's a $10,000 limit. Because of the nature of your business or your lifestyle, you run it up to $9,000 every month, but you pay it off every month. Okay?

I can't tell you how many people come to me and say, "I've got a 680 credit score, I don't understand. I have perfect this and this." Okay you're paying it off every month. Here's the important part and this is so critical. Let's say that day 1 represents the day that your billing cycle starts.

David:　　Okay.

Doc:　　Or that they send you the bill, you've got until say the 25th to make this payment. Well, they know that most people are going to make that payment somewhere in that 21st to 24th day, right? Maybe the day of the 25th. A lot of times these credit card companies will report on the 19th. If you can imagine if that guy who runs his credit card up to $9,000 on a $10,000 limit when they report you on the 19th you may have an $8,500 balance or a $9,000 balance. Well, it doesn't matter that you paid it off on the 21st, because what they reported is that highest possible balance in the span of that billing cycle. Essentially what's happening is for a month they're reporting you are being at $9,000, you're at 90% of your available limit.

David:　　Yep.

Doc:　　It makes you looked maxed out and we all know what happens to your credit score when that happens. What you can do is number 1, call your credit card company and ask them, so say, "What day does this report to all 3 bureaus?" Believe it or not, they'll tell you. If they don't tell you, call back and get somebody else on the phone. Call until you find out who it is because they can tell you. You go and it reports on the 19th, pay it on the 17th. Pay it online so there's no question about the delay or when it gets there. Don't ever send checks to credit card companies, it's a terrible idea. "Oh, we lost it in the mail."

David:　　Right, of course you did, yeah.

Doc:　　Pay it on the 17th. Well, now what's your balance going to be on the 19th when they report?

David: Nothing.

Doc: It's going to be at its absolute lowest for the month. You're going to immediately begin using it again on the 20th or the 21st. You can run it all the way up to $9,000 again, but if you pay it right before they report you're still going to look like an absolute hero with virtually no credit utilization. That ratio is going to be spectacular and before you know they're going to be doing what they did to me, which is raising your credit limits every time you turn around.

David: Right.

Doc: That cycle is beneficial because now whatever balances I do carry and allow to report it's on a much higher limit, so the percentage is still much lower. That's a very positive thing. You can actually ask to have your payment date changed. They're more likely to change your payment date, than they are the report date. You can have the due date changed and then you just avoid the whole thing all together.

David: Oh that's really cool.

Doc: I've literally seen guys that have $100,000 in available lines of credit. They've got a 680 credit score. This is a true story. I had a guy that he bought cars with his, I think it was $150,000 Amex at the auction. He bought high end cars, Mercedes, Lexus and so on. He was essentially a broker. He would just find a car that somebody wanted and he would go buy it and bring it to them and he'd make $5,000-$10,000 a pop on the sale of that vehicle. He had 1 or 2 not paying the way they were supposed to or whatever, so the first time reports it shows him as having $120,000 balance on his $150,000 line. Well, that's the first time that it happened and all of a sudden the bank starts freaking out because his score drops. The first thing they start doing, is cutting his lines.

David: Oh! man.

Doc: Now, he doesn't have the buying power that he had before and Wells Fargo and I will put them on glass for this because

I've seen them do it more times than I care to recall. You have a $5,000 line, you've been carrying a $4,000 balance, $4,500 balance for 3 years and then all of a sudden you get a raise or you get a windfall of some kind of cash, a scratch off ticket or something and you pay it down to $500, Wells Fargo will immediately lower your credit limit to 2 grand.

David: Wow.

Doc: You go from being at 90% unused on that $5,000 line down to 50% unused credit on a $2,000 line. You're worse off than you might have been before, it happens all the time.

David: It's crazy. All right. Who should contact you? Who is the maybe ideal client that you can help the most?

Doc: Essentially anybody that has been declined anything. Trying to buy a mortgage and you can't do so because of the collection activity, the charge offs, the late payments, bankruptcy, foreclosure, judgment, any of that stuff. We may or may not be able to help and I don't want to say that we can help everybody.

David: Right.

Doc: We usually can help I'd say a very high percentage, but there's probably 10% we have to turn away because we're not the right option for them but we'll send them to someone, whether it's bankruptcy or something else. That's the ideal. The other segment of this and this is very, very important. Back in 2004-2006 you had a 580 credit score and a pulse. Fog a mirror... that was the joke, if you fog a mirror, you could get a loan. Well, back then it was just about getting people to qualify. Well, then I remember when they raised the score to 600 and people thought the bottom of the world was going to fall out. "Oh, this is not going to work, oh what are we going to do?" Well, of course, they raise the standards and people had to work a little harder to keep their credit in good shape and then it went to 620, then 640 and oh my goodness it was Armageddon.

David: Right, of course it was.

Doc: Well, people get used to it and now we're building back up to that and people are managing their credit, the economy is infinitely better. Now, it's not just about qualifying. You've got people that are already a 640 but if they get to a 680 a few more doors open like we talked about before. Because those doors open, this client now can do a couple of different things. Number 1, if they lower their interest rate by a percentage on a $200,000 house well that frees up a lot of money in the monthly payment. Now, you can either use that money and just save it, put into retirement, put it into investments, college funds or whatever, or you can actually now afford maybe a slightly larger house. Maybe you get a 3 car garage instead of 2, maybe you get the polished nickel fixtures as opposed to the cheesy looking brass ones or just whatever it is.

It allows people to not only qualify but to qualify for more, and qualify for better. I don't want to say that it's only if you have a 580 credit score call us, or a 500 credit score call us. If you've got a 640 and you'd like to get into another echelon of homes, a little more for your money that's just as great a client. Likewise the example, I used before doctor, lawyer, white collar executive, somebody that's making a ton of money, and they want to buy a million dollar house. Well every 8th of a point on that interest rate matters and if I can just look at the report. It may not even require any action on my part, hiring me, or anything. I can just look at the report and say, "Hey look, here's something you can do." Maybe that last tip I shared about paying before reporting.

David: Oh yeah, that alone.

Doc: That can take a lot of people from, particularly as they get higher scores that can take somebody from 720-740-760 pretty quickly. That's extremely advantageous and that's a really useful tool for mortgage people and for real estate people in general because that's the kind of tip that, it's like "Look, I don't have to send to credit repair. I'm going to tell you something to do."

If you know you're going to buy a million dollar house in 2 months, here's what I want you to do for the next 2 months. Pay this before this date and so on and so forth, you're obviously going to look like an absolutely hero, not only did you make the money on the million dollar loan, well this guys is going to go "Hey" to his buddy at the office, "I got this great mortgage guy, I've got this great realtor that showed me this awesome trick, da da da," and suddenly you're the go to guy, you're the expert. It's extremely valuable just in that regard alone.

David: Awesome, well listen thank you so much for doing the interview, this has been awesome. If you're this person, even like Doc was saying the 620-640, our lowest is 620 that we're doing HELOCs for that we found, at least that's what we're accepting as client. You may have seen in the bonus class too, we found the best HELOC that we've ever come across and we've called 111 banks now but the minimum score is 700. If you're one of our clients and you've got a HELOC or you're getting HELOC and you're in the 640 range try to get it to 700. There's a lot more benefits with the All-In-One HELOC that we offer. That's just one thing that you could benefit from of doing that.

Again, thank you so much for doing the interview this has been great, I've learned a ton and I know our members will learn a ton as well.

Doc: As I said in the beginning man, I'm always happy to do good things for good people and I'm very honored to have been given this opportunity to share a little bit.

About Doc Compton

Doc Compton is one of the nation's foremost authorities on credit repair and credit restoration. With two decades of experience in consumer credit and credit repair, he has helped thousands of people regain control of their financial futures by correcting or deleting inaccurate and incomplete information from their credit reports with each of the major credit bureaus, thus increasing their credit scores. A consumer advocate at heart, he works tirelessly to protect consumers' rights, making sure that creditors, collection agencies, and the credit bureaus are held accountable for what they report.

Made in the USA
Charleston, SC
25 August 2016